T0171638

JON

John Oliver Nelson
And the Movement for Power in the Church

Rita M. Yeasted, SFCC

iUniverse, Inc.
Bloomington

JON
John Oliver Nelson And the Movement for Power in the Church

iUniverse books may be ordered through booksellers or by contacting:

iUniverse
1663 Liberty Drive
Bloomington, IN 47403
www.iuniverse.com
1-800-Authors (1-800-288-4677)

Because of the dynamic nature of the Internet, any Web addresses or links contained in this book may have changed since publication and may no longer be valid. The views expressed in this work are solely those of the author and do not necessarily reflect the views of the publisher, and the publisher hereby disclaims any responsibility for them.

ISBN: 978-1-4502-7426-5 (sc)
ISBN: 978-1-4502-7424-1 (e)
ISBN: 978-1-4502-7425-8 (dj)

Library of Congress Control Number: 2010917401

Printed in the United States of America

iUniverse rev. date: 1/27/2012

In Memory of Rustum Roy

"Go to the people. Live with them.
Learn from them. Love them.

Start with what they know.
Build with what they have.

But with the best leaders,
when the work is done,
the task accomplished,
the people will say
'We have done this ourselves'."

~ Lao Tzu ~

(Inscription on the Christian Medical College
and Hospital of Vellore, South India.)

Author's Note and Acknowledgments

After John Oliver Nelson died in 1990, a group of his friends gathered the materials in his home at Kirkridge and diligently sorted out boxes of letters and books, publications and photographs. Within those boxes itemized by Bill Rolph and stored in Rev. Ernie Hawk's basement were thirty years of tiny 2-1/2 x 4-inch diaries with printing so small that one needed a magnifying glass to read them.

Professor Rustum Roy, a friend of Jack's for decades, and the Sycamore Community at Penn State, yearned to do something to honor JON (as he signed his letters), and they asked me if I would write his biography. While I was interested, and knew and admired Jack, my full-time position at La Roche College as Professor of English and department head allowed me scant leisure to take on this task. After refusing three times, I finally told Rustum and Ernie that I would do it - if there was not a time limit.

I never dreamed it would take me over a decade to complete, but it was written mainly during the summers, with a sabbatical trip to Yale Divinity School and a visit with Jack's sister-in-law, Jerry Nelson. I also visited Kirkridge and enjoyed the hospitality of Director Cindy Crowner, who allowed me a few days to interview those who remembered Jack and to explore the archives. Over the years, the story of John Oliver Nelson, Yale Divinity Professor and founder of the Protestant Retreat Movement was discovered in those boxes of material, the minuscule diary entries, and the taped interviews. Somehow it seems ironically appropriate that a Catholic Sister would resurrect, write, and honor the life and legacy of this ecumenically astute Presbyterian clergyman.

Rustum Roy and the Sycamore Community not only provided the funds for the completion of this book, but they were an invaluable resource and support throughout the entire process. I dedicate this book especially to Rustum and to Ernie Hawk, both of whom knew Jack since the earliest days of Kirkridge and served on the Board of Directors. Their oral history of those years, next to the diaries, provided much of the material for this book. I am grateful to Kathy Mourant, a member of the Sycamore Community, who provided hospitality when I stayed at State College to interview Jack's friends.

Thanks also go to Jack's niece, Sheila Hourihan, with whom I have been in almost constant contact since the inception of this biography. Her memories of the Nelson family, and especially of Jack and Jane Nelson, provided much of the family history in the book. While I did not meet him personally, I am also grateful to John Nelson, Jack's nephew, who allowed me to spend a day at his Connecticut home reading letters belonging to his deceased father, Wenley Nelson, Jack's older brother, who died shortly after I began the book. In August of 2008, I flew to Saskatoon, Saskatchewan, and visited with Georgina Bone and Margaret Leaker, Jane's sisters, and their stories and perspective allowed me to complete the book.

There are others without whom the book would never have been completed. Dr. Christine Abbott, my colleague at La Roche, was not only a faithful and expert reader of the drafts, but she was the "wind beneath my wings." When I was ready to abandon the project, Chris repeatedly promised that together we would finish it—and we did. And I cannot forget the friends who encouraged me to complete the biography when I experienced the death of my parents, who did not live to see its completion: Father Vernon Holtz, OSB, whose support never wavered; and Shirley, Barb, Carolyn, Janine, and Linda—I thank them all for being there.

No list of acknowledgments would be complete without also thanking Dr. Heather McKinney, who served as managing editor of the book, acted as a liaison with the publisher, and did the final editing and formatting. All errors are mine alone.

And finally thank you to Jean Richardson, the current Director of Kirkridge, who has been both encouraging and helpful. Her dedication to Kirkridge and her desire to keep Jack's vision alive inspired me to get this book printed and into the Kirkridge Book Nest.

***

Kirkridge remains vibrant. Information about upcoming events at Kirkridge may be found at **www.kirkridge.org**. All proceeds from the sale of this book benefit Kirkridge.

Contents

2. Nelson Family Portrait: Margaret Dodds Nelson, Wenley
Nelson, Douglas Nelson, John Oliver Nelson, John Evon
Nelson, Margaret (Peggy) Nelson – early 1920's

Prologue

Shortly before noon on June 15, 1995, I made a call to Homewood Cemetery in the East End of Pittsburgh. I had been gathering material for a biography of John Oliver Nelson for about a year, and having just received a copy of his will, I noted that he asked to be buried in the family plot there, not far from his childhood home. Wanting to see his grave site, I asked Janet Kettering, secretary of Homewood Cemetery, if she could give me information about the location of Jack's grave.

"Is this the minister?" she asked. Pleasantly surprised that she would know of Jack, I immediately answered yes.

"He isn't buried here," she replied.

I patiently explained that she must be mistaken because his wish had definitely been to be buried in Homewood near his parents.

"No, I'm sure I'm right," she insisted. "His ashes are here, but they aren't buried."

Confused and stunned, I tried to comprehend how John Oliver Nelson, scion of one of Pittsburgh's most prominent Presbyterian families, Princeton *bon vivant*, Edinburgh and McCormick seminarian, Yale Ph.D., High Church executive, Yale Professor, founder of the nation's first Protestant retreat center, Kirkridge, and national leader for a subtle re-empowering of the Church in our culture. . .could it be that *this* Jack Nelson had never been buried? I could only listen as Kettering recounted what would become one of the most telling stories of Jack Nelson's life and death.

"One Saturday afternoon a few years ago, I was working in the office," Kettering explained, "when an Asian gentleman came asking for directions to Rev. Nelson's grave site." She went on to describe how the man had come to America solely to visit the grave, and it was clear she'd wanted to accommodate him. Removing the Nelson file from the safe, however, she discovered that while John Oliver Nelson had directed he be buried in the family plot, his ashes had never been sent for burial.

When the gentleman asked where they were now, Kettering was unable to answer his question. She phoned Jack's niece in Rhode Island and discovered that she had the cremains in her home. Sheila Hourihan explained that she'd hoped to bury her Uncle Jack's ashes together with his wife Jane's, but her inability to obtain Jane's death (1981) certificate from Canada had kept things frozen for more than a decade.

Kettering's story continued. "The man asked me how to get to Rhode Island," she said; "he was a bit irate, and I quieted him by making arrangements with Sheila to meet him at a Rhode Island bus station with Jack's ashes.

"He told me he'd be back next year," said Kettering, "and he wanted to see Dr. Nelson's ashes buried when he arrived."

I pictured this man sitting in the bus station for hours holding the small black box containing Jack's ashes. Sheila sent Jack's ashes to Homewood Cemetery with a check to cover the cost of burial. When they arrived, Janet Kettering remembered how deeply this minister was loved by the man from abroad. She couldn't have known that the man had once lived at Kirkridge with the Nelsons, but she did decide to hold the ashes in the basement vault until the man returned so that he could participate in a quiet burial ceremony.

But the man never came back. The box containing Jack's ashes sat for three years in the basement vault of Homewood Cemetery, forgotten. Only Janet Kettering knew the story, and luckily, she was the one to answer the phone that fateful Thursday afternoon when I called.

When she discovered I was writing a biography of Dr. Nelson, she asked if I would like to be a part of burying his ashes. "Of course," I replied without hesitation. On September 23, 1995, having found a death certificate for Jane Bone Nelson, friends arranged a grave side memorial service for these two remarkable persons. That is how the story ends. This is how it began.....

Birth to Brentwood

1909-1940

The biggest news in Pittsburgh, Pennsylvania the second week of May, 1909, was not the birth of John Oliver Nelson. That dubious honor went to the Ohio River tragedy of Tuesday, May 11, when an overloaded gasoline launch carrying 28 workers home from the Pressed Car Company sank mid-river while crossing from McKees Rocks to Woods Run. The 23 men who drowned, most of them under 30, were among Pittsburgh's poorest: immigrants with neither insurance nor benefits, sons of widowed mothers, young husbands and fathers. By week's end relief efforts expanded throughout the city.

John Oliver Nelson, born on May 14, 1909, was only two generations away from the poverty of these ill-fated laborers. His grandfather, Ambrose Nelson, had arrived in America from Scotland in 1880, bringing with him his wife Elizabeth Forsythe, a daughter Margaret, and an infant son, John Evon.

The City Directories from 1882-85 list Ambrose Nelson's occupation as stone cutter, but from 1887-98, he is listed as a city missionary, a street preacher. In 1967 when the Nelson estate was donated to the Pittsburgh Theological Seminary, Donald G. Miller sent Jack a black book containing enrollment cards dating back to the 1880s and some sermon manuscripts with a note explaining that these were probably his grandfather's notes.

3. John Oliver Nelson at 5 years old

Shortly after the family's arrival in the United States, their son and daughter were joined by three more sisters: Elizabeth, Mary Forsythe, and Edith. In November of 1898 Elizabeth Forsythe Nelson was widowed, leaving her with four daughters at home. John Evon, Jack's father, attended Park Institute and graduated from Westminster College at New Wilmington in 1900 when he was 20.

After two years with the old Keystone National Bank, John was asked by Andrew W. Mellon if he could type. "No," he answered, "but I could learn in two weeks." He did–and within a short time he was promoted from his position of bank clerk to Andrew Mellon's secretary. John went on to become vice-president, treasurer, and board member of Gulf Oil Corporation, and the family benefited from increasing income. Three of John's sisters became school teachers. On September 6, 1905, in Michigan, John married Margaret Dodds, a Methodist minister's daughter, giving John Oliver Nelson a ministerial heritage from two grandfathers. Jack's mother attended the Pennsylvania College for Women in Pittsburgh (now Chatham

University) and graduated in philosophy from the University of Michigan. An accomplished musician, Mrs. Nelson gave music lessons from her home; over time piano recitals and teas became common occurrences in the Nelson parlor (a parlor that comfortably housed three grand pianos).

Jack had an older brother, Wenley Dodds Nelson, with whom he was always close. When Jack was four, a second brother, Douglas Evon, was born, and three years later Margaret Elizabeth (Peggy) completed the family. They were the only grandchildren of Elizabeth Nelson and the darlings of four Nelson aunts: Margaret (Marnie), Elizabeth (Bess), Mary (Massa), and Edith (Edie). Like Jack, Douglas went into the ministry, and after fulfilling his first pastorate in Texas, he became pastor at a Presbyterian church in New Haven, Connecticut. Wenley followed in his father's footsteps by going into business, and Peggy married the famed composer Howard Hanson.

Each of the Nelson children played a musical instrument, and it was commonplace for the family to entertain guests and themselves. In a **Post-Gazette** article dated March 28, 1931, Mrs. Nelson described a musical family trio consisting of her piano, John Oliver's first violin, and Wenley's cello. Friends were encouraged to use the Nelson music room and to make use of the instruments there, "a cello, two violas, three violins, a cornet, and a real Scottish bagpipe," a recently acquired possession sent home by Jack from Scotland, where he was attending the University of Edinburgh.

Jack, his brothers, and sister enjoyed a far more comfortable life than did their father's family. Summers were spent at Chautauqua, where their mother, Margaret, had spent her own summers (a Nelson summer home still sits on the lake). Even through the Depression, the Nelsons did not feel the pinch as sharply as so many others. Family members tell stories of the Nelson men walking to church on Sunday in top hats and cutaways, and of how Jack's pet monkey once got loose and the family chauffeur had to pick Jack up at school to catch it.

The three boys were active in youth groups. Jack committed himself to the YMCA (Young Men's Christian Association) as a young man, and went on to work for the National Office as an adult. The brothers were also active in the young people's groups of their church. Wenley, graduating from Schenley High School, attended public schools his entire life, while Jack left Schenley for Shady Side Academy to complete his senior year. On every vitae John Oliver Nelson listed himself as a 1926 graduate of Shady Side Academy, a prestigious academy for young men from wealthy families. The school yearbook lists his membership in the Gargoyle Club, the glee club, the St. Andrew's Society, and the Seven Arts Club. In fact, the short biography accompanying Jack's photograph provides an interesting insight into his future career:

> Aside from fiddling, drawing, acting, and studying, John, better known as "Jack", has nothing to do. If you meet him on the campus, he is either looking for somebody or going someplace. He has a rather good voice, as is evidenced by his work in the Glee Club. Probably the climax of his career at Shady Side came when he strutted his stuff in "A Full House."
>
> When it came to fiddling, Jack could give Nero a run for his money. His real ambition in this line is, however, to play in the Triangle Club. His artistic ability is the source of several of the plates in this book. His appetite is equaled only by that of his room-mate. Considering all he has done for the school, we shall be sorry to lose him; but we wish him the best of luck in Princeton. (p. 80)

As predicted, in the fall of 1926 Jack joined Wenley, already a senior, at Princeton. Jack's undergraduate years, described in family letters, were happy and rewarding. John Evon Nelson sent his sons a letter almost every day they were at school, and while few of his letters to Jack remain, Wenley's letters show a father who cared deeply for his sons, sometimes reminding Wenley to look out for his younger brother–and, if family stories are true, Jack sometimes needed looking after. His high school dream of joining the Triangle Club was realized; Jack performed with this musical group on and off campus, often for college musical productions.

4. 5.

6. Jack as a student during Princeton years (1926-1930)

Jack reveled in the social life at Princeton. A favorite family story recounts how Jack and a few of his friends stole the gong from the bell in the college bell tower, and how he kept it on the wall for years as a memento of his days at Princeton. Both known as "ladies' men," Wenley and Jack were often invited to formal teas and debutante balls in New York and at the university, and on one occasion, having missed the last train back to New Jersey, the weary brothers slept on Pennsylvania Station benches—tuxedos and all.

Mr. Nelson's letters chide Jack's request for money to procure a raccoon coat that he absolutely had to have, and it's doubtful that the elder Nelson would have approved the purchase of standing ash trays for both boys' dormitory rooms. A rather interesting letter was written on the 11th of October 1926, wherein Wenley tells his father --addressed as Dr. Mr. Nelson--that Jack wasn't "doing any smoking at all, or indulging in any of the other campus sins."

Jack's seeming conversion might be explained partially by his affiliation with the Princeton Campus Crusaders. Founded in 1912, the Crusaders consisted of upperclassmen, invited to join by the Director, dedicating themselves "to God's will for themselves and the world." Jack's affiliation with this group persisted throughout his life. Members were asked to attend an annual Service of Dedication at commencement, and in the prayer they said each year may be found the language and seeds of the Kirkridge vision, an experiment that would bloom twelve years after Jack's graduation from Princeton. In fact, it was at Princeton that the first discussions of the formation of a "dedicated order" similar to Iona took place.

In an era when the Grand Tour of Europe was expected of wealthy young men, younger brother Doug, 16, and Jack, 20, traveled to Paris and Scotland the summer before Jack's senior year. Doug's widow remembered how the two bought gifts for all the girls they met in their travels–and Doug had to carry them because he had taken fewer clothes than Jack for the journey.

Everyone assumed journalism would be Jack's chosen career path, so it's intriguing to speculate as to how he ended up in the ministry. Various theories exist. With two grandfathers in ministry, one of whom Jack would have known as a child, and having been reared in a devout Presbyterian family, his father an elder in the church, the path does not seem that unusual.

Yet Jack's family tells the story that during his years at Princeton, while working on a banana boat one summer, he fell into the water and had a "conversion experience" that changed his life. Whether this family legend is true or not, what is known is that upon graduation, Jack went to New College, University of Edinburgh. Jack's path to the ministry was sealed when he met George MacLeod, a Church of Scotland minister, with a parish in Govan, a Depression-devastated district in Glasgow.

While MacLeod would not begin the rebuilding of the Abbey on Iona until 1938, seeing the dire poverty of many of his out-of-work parishioners led him to employ them to rebuild a ruined village mill, which eventually became a community center. Encouraged by this success, MacLeod was inspired to rebuild the ruins of Iona, a tiny island among the Inner Hebrides off the southwest tip of Mull.

Iona was established in May 563 when St. Columba and twelve fellow monks arrived from the north of Ireland. Like his earlier Irish counterpart, St. Patrick, Columba brought Celtic Christianity to Scotland. From this blessed isle, sacred even in pre-Christian times, monks set sail in small boats to establish Christianity in the British Isles and as far south as Vienna.

A center for scholarship and holiness, Iona saw the beginning of the illustrated Book of Kells, Ireland's most famous medieval relic. In the thirteenth century a Benedictine abbey and small cathedral dedicated to Mary were built on the island, and although reformers dismantled the site in 1561, Iona was held in reverence by Christians for centuries.

No one knows for sure on what date in 1931 Jack Nelson first met George MacLeod, but we do know that as a young divinity student, Jack was inspired by the Scottish minister for whom the Gospel demanded more than mere lip service. With the success of the rebuilt mill, MacLeod's vision extended to Iona, where in 1938 he, like St. Francis before him, decided to rebuild a church. For MacLeod this inner call to reform and rebuild not only demanded a change of heart and a concrete commitment to act beyond mere church attendance, but also a radical vision to create a new social order.

The first twelve workers at Iona included six unemployed craftsmen from MacLeod's parish and six seminarians. Lacking funds, MacLeod petitioned Sir James Lithgos, a builder of warships at his Govan shipyard to give him £5,000. When asked if MacLeod would give up his pacifism in return, the minister responded, "Not on your life." Impressed with his integrity, Lithgos replied, "Then I will give you your £5,000."

The ties that link Iona and Kirkridge abound. We know, for instance, that Jack helped to lay slate tiles on the roof of the Abbey refectory one summer and that he participated in the early, austere years of this fledgling "summer community." Seminarians worked on the construction during summer vacation, and craftsmen would stay on the island as autumn grew into winter until the weather became too brutal. Eventually a community emerged, a new monastic life formed around the rebuilt abbey. Obligations were fourfold and included:

- Common life–several months of experience working at the abbey and at least one week together each year on the island.
- Common discipline–daily reading of Scripture and at least a half hour of prayer at set morning and evening times.
- Participation at meetings–regional meetings and one annual meeting at Iona itself.

- Commitment to peace and non-violence–a remarkable decision since the community was founded during World War II.

The ecumenical nature of this venture is deeply rooted. The cradle of Celtic Christianity, Iona evolved into a Roman Catholic Benedictine presence. Many of the early monks were martyred, and many others left the island for safer shores. With the Protestant Reformation, all traces of Roman Catholicism were driven underground. Iona, left abandoned for four centuries, fell into ruin.

According to a 1947 brochure, in 1910 the Duke of Argyll gave the ruins back to the Church of Scotland as "Trustees for all Christendom" so that the church might be rebuilt. He expressed the hope that "any recognized denomination might seek, and be granted, the use of the restored Abbey for the full office of its worship," thus becoming "the only church in Christendom that every denomination can call 'Home.'"

MacLeod's dream was not only to rebuild an abbey, but to fulfill the prophecy made by St. Columba a thousand years before:

In Iona of my heart, Iona of my love,
Instead of monks' voices shall be lowing of cattle,
But, ere the world come to an end,
Iona shall be as it was.

The decidedly ecumenical nature of Iona, its passion for social justice for the poor, and its concern for liturgical renewal, all would have attracted John Oliver Nelson.

Jack's year of theological studies at Edinburgh University culminated in a divinity degree from Chicago's McCormick Seminary in 1933. That same year Jack Nelson headed off to Yale Divinity School to complete his doctorate. He defended his dissertation, ***The Rise of the Princeton Theology: A Genetic Study of American Presbyterianism Until 1850***, in the spring of 1935 and applied to the Presbyterian Board for a pastorate. Advised in his senior interview at Yale to get a church of his own, however small, Jack found himself the fourth pastor of Brentwood Presbyterian Church, a small mission church of Shadyside Presbyterian, the Nelson family's home church.

7. The John Evon Nelson Family ~ 1932. Wenley Dodds Nelson, John Oliver Nelson, Margaret Elizabeth Nelson, Margaret Nora Dodds Nelson, Douglas Evon Nelson.

In *Fishers of Men*, a history of Brentwood Presbyterian published for its 40th anniversary in 1969, Fred Weaver tells of how Dr. Nelson drove his Ford daily from Brentwood to East End, where he lived with his parents. That trip in 1935 was not an easy one, nor was becoming pastor to a church of 200 members, who met in a concrete block structure that had seen little improvement since its recent construction.

The church had not yet been fully paid for, which led Pastor Nelson to depend upon financial help from Shadyside. Ordained and installed on July 19, 1935, Jack Nelson brought the passion and energy that would characterize his whole life to make Brentwood Presbyterian a church that would attract both young and old. A few members still recall his amazing achievements. In the historian's prophetic words, "under his direction the Church immediately began to move."

Brentwood, Pennsylvania, today, with the beautiful Presbyterian church still sitting on the corner of Brownsville Road and Hillman Street, is a far cry from the small town in the South Hills of Pittsburgh in which Jack first ministered. Arriving in the midst of the Depression, Jack found many in his church out of work, yet a core of dedicated men and women met his challenge to reorganize the Sunday school, begin a church bulletin, start a choir, and initiate plans for a new building.

The original sketches for the present church were made by John Oliver Nelson, and his initials can still be seen on the pen and ink drawings in the church archives. Motivated by his love for music (especially good choral music), Jack was determined to provide an organ for the church. Finding a $20 reed organ in a theater, Jack used a Hoover sweeper suction blower to reanimate the aging instrument, and soon the church boasted both organ and organist. Having no real pulpit, Jack had a five-sided podium built from five paneled kitchen doors. He organized a joint Easter sunrise service in Brentwood Park with a trumpet call across the ravine, illustrating the love of liturgy that would characterize his whole life.

What the Brentwood Presbyterian members interviewed most recalled was Jack's commitment to young people. In what is now Castle Shannon, a neighboring community on Route 88, the Mollenauer Mining Settlement was filled with children living in poverty with few outlets for play or creative activity. Jack asked the Men's Club to begin a Mollenauer Mission to help the boys from this area, many of whom had dropped out of school to work in the mines and had spent some time at Morganza, Thorn Hill, and other juvenile correctional schools. A boisterous, vulgar, poker-playing and swearing Club, the boys wanted no strangers interfering with their coarse hideout. But Jack would not be daunted. In a short time, he learned that they enjoyed singing, so they sang "not always in tune, but loud" to begin every meeting.

Soon some of the boys agreed to read familiar parts of the Bible or a prayer for the meetings, and in time "Doc Nelson" (whom most never suspected was a minister) developed a friendship with the boys, even inviting them to his home at 201 N. Murtland Avenue in Pittsburgh's East End. Athel P. Rowles remembers that one of the ring-leaders, flaunting his physical prowess, challenged "Doc" to a wrestling match, not realizing that the Nelsons had a full gym in their home and that Jack made regular use of it. "In less than three minutes the challenger was being bounced about like a rubber ball," Rowles writes, and after about 18 months with the boys, the Juvenile Court of Allegheny County reported that the number of cases out of Mollenauer had dropped to a point that the Court "wondered whether the 'Patch' had been torn down or burned out" (*Fishers,* 41).

Jack's five years at Brentwood Presbyterian Church crackled with energy and forecast many of his lifelong passions. The founding of Brentminster Fellowship, an active youth group in the parish, provided an opportunity both to train lay church leaders and to promote rousing hymn singing at the church, allowing Jack's musical talent to be put to good use. His 1936 diary tells, for example, of his help with the Brentminster production of *Daniel and the Scribe.* The young people attended summer camps and conferences, often at Jack's expense, and as noted in *Fishers of Men,* "Brentminster was addressed by a Negro minister, and later as clouds of World War II gathered, their speaker was a Presbyterian minister whose theme [was] pacifism with strong overtones of conscientious objection to military service" (31).

Jack organized a softball team, a Cub Scout Pack, a "Summer College" and Community Forum at the local high school, and from 1935 until he left in 1940, the Church School increased from 250 members and teachers to 572. The church itself was enlarged with the financial support of Shadyside Presbyterian. The Schultz property next to the church was purchased for $7,000 in 1937, and the congregation voted to erect an addition to the south of the building and remodel the existing structure.

In December of 1938, Brentwood Presbyterian was rededicated, dissolving the relationship with Shadyside and able to stand on its own. Jack's first five-year position ended on June 30, 1940. Under his leadership, the church had become self-supporting, "sending more delegates to summer conferences than any other Church in the Presbytery" (***Fishers*** 36). Four young men of the community entered the ministry during Jack's pastorate, and while "he himself disclaimed credit for the decisions of three of them, there are those who were then in the Youth Group who are convinced that by word and example [Jack] guided and encouraged them in the progress of their studies" (***Fishers*** 37).

Jack Nelson left Brentwood for Philadelphia in 1940 to begin his work with the Board of Christian Education of the Presbyterian Church in the U.S.A., a position that put him in contact with seminarians and seminary directors throughout the country. In addition, he traveled to Scotland, where his affiliation with the Iona Community House in Glasgow became such a bedrock of his spirituality that it fortified his dream to set up an "American Iona," a desire that in 1942 would become Kirkridge.

The Dream Realized: "Seed-Bed" for New Life

1940-1950

Jack Nelson never tired of telling the anecdote of how when he purchased the diamond-shaped acreage on the Appalachian Trail that would become Kirkridge, residents of Bangor, Pennsylvania, chuckled: "This city fellow is really getting took. There hasn't been a decent potato crop on the property for the past ten years." But it wasn't potatoes that interested John Oliver Nelson; it was a new vision for the Church.

Having met George MacLeod in 1931 while a seminary student at Edinburgh, Jack Nelson was inspired to rethink the role of the Church in the world. As he explained in a recorded interview in 1989, there was a growing movement in Europe, especially the Low Countries, to revitalize the Church after the First World War.

While in Scotland, Jack, through George MacLeod, was introduced to Talbot House and TOC H, begun during World War I in Belgium. He affiliated himself with their stated goal of "building a fairer society by working with communities to promote friendship and service, confront prejudice, and practise reconciliation," and became a member. Having studied at Yale Divinity School the writings of Anglican Bishop Charles Gore, founder of the Community of Resurrection at Mirfield, Jack saw the importance of blending

14

theology with a social conscience. He learned of the efforts of ecumenical Archbishop Nathan Söderblom of Sigtuna, Sweden, who gathered church leaders from many different traditions to Uppsala and Stockholm in 1925, addressing the responsibility of the churches for world peace.

Jack also became acquainted with Brother Roger, founder of France's Taizé Community (1940), whose first mission was aiding Jewish refugees during the war. An early supporter of the Fellowship of Reconciliation (FOR), founded in Switzerland in 1914, Jack eventually served as Chairman of this interfaith and international movement. Each of these threads ultimately became woven into the vision that would become Kirkridge.

After leaving Brentwood Presbyterian and beginning his work with the Department of Student Relations of the Presbyterian Board of Christian Education in Philadelphia, Jack continued to explore peacemaking efforts during the Second World War, still on the European front in 1940. During the War, he was active with advising conscientious objectors. Once Kirkridge was established, Jack often drove these COs, who worked 12-hour shifts in Philadelphia's mental hospitals as alternative service, to the mountains for their one day off.

But it was Iona's vision that most captured Jack's heart. In his travels across the country as part of his job at 820 Witherspoon, Jack kept in contact with like-minded ministers, especially those Presbyterians with whom he worked. By 1941 he felt the need to form an American Iona, and began to share this idea with close friends Bob Giffen of the Westminster Foundation at Princeton and Laurence T. Hosie, Director of the Labor Temple on Fourteenth Street and Second Avenue, New York, a Presbyterian organization with an outreach to workers.

When Jack told the story of how Kirkridge came to be, he reminded listeners that the first choice for this visionary center was an island in the Susquehanna River, but the one offered by a couple in Columbia, Pennsylvania, was under water twice a year, so the second choice was a mountain retreat. Seeking a place equidistant from Philadelphia and New York, where most of the interested men lived and worked, he wrote to real estate agents in the region of the Pocono Mountains.

In early April he drove his Model A Ford to Stroudsburg. While looking at small parcels of land in the area with Dale Learn, a Methodist deacon, Jack looked up at the land on the Kittatinny Ridge and asked if this land was available. Not wanting to seem uninformed, Mr. Learn quickly explained that this property was very expensive, and the owners would never part with it. But a few days after Jack returned to Philadelphia, he received a call from the embarrassed realtor, who explained that after checking out the property, he learned that the owners of the Landon property would be willing to sell, and at a price that might be agreeable.

Jack jumped at the chance to put a down payment on it, and when the first group of "hungry men" met at Princeton on May 14, 1942, they decided unanimously to go ahead with the purchase and the dream.

The wooded ridge that caught Jack's eye (and heart) lay 85 miles straight north of Philadelphia and 85 miles straight west of New York. Its 350 acres along the Appalachian Trail contained an "1815 sharecroppery farmhouse," a brook, outbuildings, 50 acres of fields, and springs so pure that early in the century farmers lined up to get water for their car batteries.

The property also contained a high knoll with a superb view, where the Nelson Lodge now stands, 1,540 feet above sea level and about five miles from Stroudsburg, Pennsylvania. Delighted at his find, he asked a few of his colleagues to join him to look over the property, and on April 13 Jack and Bob Giffen went to look over the property and its possibilities. Jack paid the $500 down payment on the property out of his own pocket, using "thrift stamps from my kindergarten days during the First World War."

The first important meeting of those interested in this project for a "dedicated order within the ministry" was held at Princeton on May 14, Jack's 33rd birthday. "Eleven of us–just a roomful at the Foundation House," Jack wrote in the Preliminary Paper of June 1, 1942: "Bob Giffen as host, Ted Rath from Clinton, New Jersey, Jim Alter and Hal Leiper from Yale, Dr. and Mrs. Richard Roberts 'from Canada and Wales,' Larry Hosie of Labor Temple, Ralph Mould of 2nd Germantown, Fay Campbell [of the Presbyterian Board] and Jack Nelson from the Witherspoon Building, and Dick Comfort from Union," men he would later describe as "social gospel firebrands."

The Preliminary Paper describes the meeting as having a "good deal of silence, close discussion, a memorable meal in the garden, and an overnight for some of us." Those present, he writes, "began the job of focusing our vision of the will of God in the movement we contemplate. Our common aim found general expression (not minutely worded) in three very simple direct sentences.

- We reaffirm our faith in God's will as it is fully revealed in Christ.
- We declare that the power of that will is among us and in us thwarted and unrealized because it is imperfectly channeled.
- We seek earnestly to rediscover ways of making God's power effective through us, in the explicit situation in which he places us: the historic Christian tradition, the Reformed faith in America, the ministry, and the intimate company of friends."

In a recorded interview of 1989 in which Jack recalled that May meeting, he explained that the first group to meet at Princeton were divided into those very involved in social action and others he described as "Quaker types." From this mix evolved the motto of Kirkridge: *Picket and Pray.*

When asked why it wasn't *Pray and Picket*, Jack explained that after much discussion, the group decided that most of them were already doing the picketing, but they were "running out of gas," and they needed the kind of depth and spirituality that would enable them to do the things that they deemed so important. Jack later explained that picketing should not be a solo effort and always had a connotation of taking an unpopular, courageous stand by people who were not in the majority. "Picketing is a *group* enterprise," he remarked during a 1981 retreat, "which will cost something sooner or later."

This pivotal meeting at 86 Stockton Street, Princeton, outlined what would be the direction of Kirkridge for the next two decades. It was here the name Kirkridge was selected, with the alternate choice being Churchcroft. "Kirk" is Scottish for church. Therefore, Kirkridge means "the Church on the Ridge."

The group decided upon a shared devotional discipline and planned for the month's training period for seminarians and a list of tasks to present to seminarians that fall. It was also decided to choose a director or farm manager as soon as possible after the property was taken over on July 1, and to incorporate as soon as possible to enable gifts to be accepted by the movement.

As Jack wrote in the Preliminary Paper, "The farm property involves no outlay for us, but improvements will." Jack withdrew an additional $2,000 from his Princeton account on May 15 to take to Stroudsburg, $500 of which was earned while he was editor of the *Princeton Tiger*, $100 of which was a birthday gift from his family. Eventually, he took out a loan for the rest of the property's cost, $11.75 per month for three years, so that Kirkridge would be paid for by 1945. In fact, records show that it was paid off by 1943.

The summer of 1942 was a buzz of activity for Jack and for these ministers he would later call "the hungry men." On June 15, twelve men joined Jack at Kirkridge. With only a farmhouse and two recently built poultry houses to serve as dormitories on the property, Jack knew that the first priority had to be to make the farmhouse livable. Four 30-inch cots and mattresses were bought from Sears, Roebuck at a cost of $10 each, plus a bathtub.

With a plan to make room for 20 by the spring, Jack got carpenters from the area to begin working on the farmhouse, knocking out two partitions to make the whole downstairs one big room, "which won't be bad when we get the joints concealed." A three-burner oil stove for cooking and running cold water provided the only other amenities. The farmhouse had a multiple-party telephone with nine subscribers at a cost of $1.25 monthly.

There was no electricity, and because it was wartime, no lines could be installed "for the duration." In addition, Jack had the group work at "deforesting an acre at the crest of the Kirkridge knoll, axing shrubs, trimming the taller trees."

Because of wartime gasoline rationing, Jack put his car in a garage in Bangor, and took trains to Kirkridge. He worked during the week for the Presbyterian Board, and spent every weekend on the mountain. He would often bring some of the early members of the Princeton group and eventually young seminarians, which over that summer expanded to quite a few men. These work retreats were the pattern for many years.

Men rose early in silence, had breakfast at 6:45 during which someone read from a spiritual book, followed by morning prayer at 7:30. Work projects began at 8 a.m., with an 11:00 return for a snack and wash-up, with discussion at 11:30 led by one of the retreatants or Jack. Dinner at 1:15 was followed by more work or rest if needed, then a 4:30 discussion, 6:30 supper, and 7:30 "hearth hour."

Compline at 8:45 began the traditional great silence of religious communities that was the gift of Quaker influence, particularly Douglas Steere of Pendle Hill. The hearth hour over the years became such an important part of the Kirkridge experience that many of those who wrote of their early Kirkridge experiences mentioned the fireplace as a sacred space, the closest thing to a chapel on the mountain.

In a letter to Bob Giffen dated July 7, Jack wrote: "Today I'm as stiff as a board (naw, not merely a Board man) from ripping the roof, slate by slate, off the most elderly of those chicken-houses, and heroically mowing the front lawn, etc." Shortly after purchasing the Landon property, Jack one summer Saturday joined the former owner, who marked the trees at the corner of his property, which the old farmer assured him was more accurate than a deed.

Having hired Paul Beidler, a "Frank Lloyd Wrightism" architect from Bethlehem, Pennsylvania, to design the future buildings of Kirkridge, Jack from the first summer of 1942 dreamed a magnificent future for this city on the hill. At the center of that vision was a chapel on the crest of the mountain, but that chapel was never built.

His dream of having a couple stay there as residents for a period of time to watch over the property would not materialize for several years, although he had hoped that Dr. and Mrs. Richard Roberts, the Canadian couple who attended the first meeting at Princeton, might decide to retire there. However, because of the war, they encountered visa problems. Not being permitted to bring any of their money out of Canada, they decided to return home. Fortunately, Dr. Roberts remained close to the project for many years.

That first summer Jack hired a Kirkridge legend–Mary E. Sullivan, known affectionately as Mayme to all who came to Kirkridge in the early days. She lived with her 89-year-old mother about a block from the farmhouse, and kept a watchful eye on all who would come near the property. Eventually, she became the cook for the early retreatants, but in her letters from that first summer, Mayme wrote to tell Jack that she mowed the lawn, picked the pears, checked on whether the taxes had been paid for the year, and, in general, saw herself as Kirkridge's on-site director. On February 23 she wrote to "Friend Nelson," as she fondly referred to JON, that the snow had drifted against the kitchen door of the farmhouse.

Since the accumulated ice was melting and running beneath the door, she shoveled the water to prevent it from going into the big room. Mayme kept the walks cleared of snow in winter and often cut the grass in the warm months. Jack loved to tell the story of how she told new retreatants of how "Me and Jack founded Kirkridge." In truth, while Jack was working during the week in Philadelphia, New York, and later at Yale, Mayme did play a very important role in the early days of Kirkridge.

By the spring of 1943, Jack, at the suggestion of his lawyer, added two incorporators to the original three to satisfy Pennsylvania corporation law. George Renneisen, head bookkeeper of the Presbyterian Board, and Larry Hosie of the Labor Temple, joined Bob Giffen, Ralph Mould, and Jack as the first legal representatives of Kirkridge. With this in place, Jack's father, John Evon Nelson gave his son a promised check for $1,500 to continue building on the property.

In a letter dated August 21, 1942, Jack wrote to his attorney, Cadmus Gordon, Jr., explaining that Kirkridge, by general consent of the early founders, would consist of a Board of Trustees, a "self-perpetuating body charged with corporate responsibility for the finances of the project," with the additional suggestion that "four ministers, with one layman who is a C.P.A. or banker, might constitute the Board and virtually the corporation itself."

In April 1943 the first official "strong-silent" farmer-caretaker was hired at the recommendation of Bob Giffen—Fred Thatcher Schurtz, described in Jack's inimitable style as "a 4-F vegetarian divorcee of considerable mechanical ability," a pacifist who would start a truck garden at once and do other needed maintenance.

An avid bike rider, Schurtz assured Jack he would not need a car, and agreed to work for $60 a month. But within a week of his hire, Fred wrote a card to Jack rethinking the absence of a car at his disposal. Fred's humor is evidenced by the closing of his letter of May 13, 1943: "Hoping this finds you more and more inclined to believe less and less." When summer began, the farmhouse had a cement bathroom in place (*sans* fixtures) behind the house, six beds ready to use, and a new front door.

The focus of Kirkridge in these early days was clear. In applying for incorporation and non-profit status, Jack wrote on August 4, 1942, to Mr. E. J. Fox, Jr., of Easton Trust: "Kirkridge is an educational and religious mutual fellowship whose purpose is to prepare pastors and pastors-to-be for specific service in underprivileged parishes of the Presbyterian Church in the U.S.A. and other communions. To this end it aims to provide and maintain a training center, whose program will include theological and social study, devotional discipline, and manual work, all under adequate direction. It aims further to foster a continuing group life among those who have taken part in this training program."

Jack and the early Kirkridge members pledged themselves to this task. In his travels across the country, Jack met with seminarians and clergy, mainly Presbyterian, but not totally. He encouraged young men to join the group during the summer and later, over Thanksgiving break. This nucleus of dedicated men hoped to make the Church come alive not only in cities, but also in the small-town and rural areas of the country, where ministers were isolated and ill-paid.

On August 28, 1942, Jack wrote in a letter to Andrew R. Towl of Wayne, Pennsylvania, that the plan for Kirkridge was to project a "training-group plan to prepare men just out of seminary for specific work in underprivileged, socially significant parishes." A kind of service corps for the Church, this movement had as its main goal to make the Gospel come alive, to take the message of Christ to the unchurched and churched alike.

In the February 1944 edition of *Atlantic Monthly*, Walter R. Clyde of Union Theological Seminary, Rio Piedras, Puerto Rico, commended the efforts of Jack and Kirkridge in his article, "Preaching in Obscurity." Dr. Clyde, the son of a country pastor, wrote of the difficulties these underpaid, isolated ministers faced. At Kirkridge, "on a mountaintop with a view of God's heaven above and God's world below," he writes, "the recruits are led by several experienced pastors in periods of discipline in worship, manual toil, and study," adding "the Kirkridge movement hopes to be a 'seed-bed' for new life among ministers: informal but earnest in discipline and intention . . . a symbol of fearless social thinking and action, grounded in manual work and life renewed in God" (81).

While Kirkridge became the center of his vision and life, Jack continued his work as director of the Life Work Department of the Presbyterian Board. The two were so closely related that when he spoke or preached at churches and colleges across the East Coast and the Midwest, the question of "vocation" was paramount for him.

Jack was a "recruiter for Christ." Notes left in a diary for these years show titles of talks that manifest his passion: "The Rediscovery of Vocation," "Planless Living is Tragedy," "Enlisting Frontiersmen," "Kingdom Harvest." In a talk at Temple University on December 4, 1942, entitled "A Ministry for Tomorrow," he discussed "three qualities I believe we shall have, and one I pray God we may have": deepened theological insight, deepened ecumenical feeling, deepened teaching programs, and finally deepened revolutionary note, spanning "revolutionary allegiance, fellowship, discipline, and direct action."

"Choose the *biggest* job you can," he told a group at Bryn Mawr in October of 1944. Ask yourself "what'll I *be*, not *do*." And because he was traveling during war time, Jack often spoke not only of a commitment to peacemaking, but to the importance of the pulpit in keeping Christians committed to their ideals. He told the story in a seminary talk he gave at least six times between 1941 and 1942 of how in a Saxon battle, the monks praying were shot at first, reminding the seminarians of the importance of keeping their parishioners focused on alternate solutions to war.

"It's up to you!" he wrote in his notes, "the whole future of mankind depends on whether we can teach this truth: 'Be not overcome by *evil*, but overcome evil with *good*.'" While "millions our age are called to overcome evil with evil," he told them, "you are ordained under the Prince of Peace to teach this nation how to overcome evil with good," adding that their job was "more important than fighting."

One of the great contributions of these early years of Kirkridge was Jack's publication of an annual lectionary (a practice that existed to recent times). This small pamphlet listed Scriptural readings and reflections for each week of the year, and every member of Kirkridge, clergy and lay, from the early 40s, received one as part of the required discipline of the members.

In the early years Jack wrote each of the lectionaries, and within the first few years, he also sent out several times a year a small pamphlet called Kirkridge *Contours*, a publication that became the impetus of many sermons not only in America, but in Scotland, where copies were sent to George MacLeod, and all over the world.

Just as Jack had served as pastor at Brentwood Presbyterian from 1935-1940, he left the Presbyterian Board of Christian Education after five years, and in 1945 began another five-year stint as Director of the Commission on the Ministry of the Federal Council of Churches (later to become the World Council of Churches) in New York City.

In a letter to "the Kirkridge Roster," dated September 28, 1945, Jack described the Work Retreat IV, held that September, in which twelve men came to Kirkridge to work and pray in preparation for their various ministries. Jack writes that discussion involved "cultivation of the 'cell,' mental healing, our Scripture lectionary, and our monthly day-of-retreat."

This reference to "cell" is very important to the early history of Kirkridge. It is also a reflection of another thread in Jack's personal history. At Princeton Jack had joined the "Crusaders"–a select group of committed Christians with roots reaching back to Frank Buchman, founder of the Oxford Group (later Moral Re-armament) whose small groups–often called cells–found their way through Henry Smith Leiper to Mao Tse-tung, his library assistant in the Peking YMCA. At one level, with a philosophy similar to that of the vigorous Communist party, these committed Christians should form "cells" of evangelical fervor, putting some of Buchman's Christian ideas–including confession–into practice.

In outlines of sermons dating from this period, we find Jack often using the example of how one Communist in a group of fifteen Christians could convert others to his beliefs, but Jack asked the question of why the fourteen did not convert the one Communist? At Ann Arbor, Michigan, in October of 1948, Jack spelled out the cell group approach, emphasizing that a retreat was needed to *start* a cell, to form fellowship, although diversity was needed within the group.

"Silence is essential to a cell," he writes, and the Bible must be the focal point of study. The discipline at the retreat consisted of five points: "up early, manual work, silence, worship, and discussion." At home, these components of the discipline would be reinforced through the cell. Lastly, social action was required. "Picket and pray," he writes, whether as a team or individually.

In the letter of September 28, mentioned above, Jack discussed the Experimental Discipline that by now was so established that the word *experimental* would be dropped. Writing that "several dozen men found it meaningful, even to sending in the report sheets," Jack decided that this discipline was "the evident core of our emphasis," and that "those who do follow the Discipline, reporting success or failure, will now qualify as the central group of Kirkridge: others, casually interested, are not so closely members of the fellowship."

Three years after its founding, Kirkridge had established a "first order" of members in this "movement for power in the Church." In a letter to Henry Luce dated January 11, 1950, Jack writes that "about one hundred men and a dozen women are sending in reports on this Rule every quarter."

The "quarterly report sheets" to which Jack refers were printed on a 5 x 8-1/2 sheet. At the top of the report was written: "This accompanies the folder, The Kirkridge Discipline, which gives rules and intentions agreed upon year by year at The Gathering (of those most earnestly concerned) at Kirkridge.

QUARTERLY REPORT SHEET
on the Kirkridge Discipline

Name .... *(JAN 1952)* .... *Custom Roy*

Three-month period: .... to .... *MAR.* ...., 19...

This accompanies the folder, The Kirkridge Discipline, which gives rules and intentions agreed upon year by year at The Gathering (of those most earnestly concerned) at Kirkridge. Marking this sheet and mailing it to Kirkridge, Bangor, Pennsylvania means not "Look at what I have achieved" but "Here is a token that I still seek to be part of our shared Christian fellowship under discipline." Another sheet will be sent you when this comes in.

Circle the days of the month when you have fulfilled the Rule.

I. To keep a daily half-hour devotion these days:
(If it is kept after 9:00, cross out the day.)

II. To read the agreed lectionary and use the agreed hymns these days:

III. To offer grace at each meal on these days:

IV. To pray at the day's end on these days:

V. To make a personal retreat each month
First Month.................... Second Month.................... Third Month....................

VI. To tithe consistently during this quarter (Check fulfillment ....)

VII. To work for growth of a Christian cell (Jot down a sentence on the reverse side of this sheet describing how.)

VIII. To share corporate church worship weekly, and an inter-church activity quarterly.

IX. To make a retreat with other Kirkridge members once yearly (Check if during this quarter ....)

PLEASE append some message overleaf before you mail this, telling what your current largest concern is, or how you have fulfilled Kirkridge Intentions as well as Rules, or anything else you want to share with the whole group at the mountain or through issues of the occasional *Ridgeleaf*.

8. Kirkridge Quarterly Report Sheet

"Marking this sheet and mailing it to *Kirkridge, Bangor, Pennsylvania* means not 'Look at what I have achieved' but 'Here is a token that I still seek to be part of our shared Christian fellowship under discipline.' Another sheet will be sent you when this comes in." On the nine-sectioned sheet one had to circle the days one kept a daily half-hour devotion, with the caveat that if it were kept after 9:00 a.m., one should *cross out* the day.

Other requirements of these first Kirkridge members were to read the agreed lectionary and use the agreed hymns daily, offer grace at each meal, pray at the day's end, make a personal retreat each month, tithe consistently during this quarter, work for growth of a Christian cell, share corporate church worship weekly, and an inter-church activity quarterly, and make a retreat with other Kirkridge members once yearly. In short, the requirements of membership for these early Kirkridge pioneers reflected both the cost of discipleship and Jack's well-founded belief that discipline was mandatory for becoming a committed Christian. If picketing did not seem to be emphasized, prayer, frugality, and sharing certainly were.

On the reverse side of the quarterly report sheet members could append some message sharing their largest concern or how they have fulfilled Kirkridge Intentions as well as Rules, or anything else they wanted "to share with the whole group at the mountain or through issues of the occasional *Ridgeleaf*." This latter publication was another of Jack's means of keeping in touch with anyone who came to Kirkridge. The newsletter is still mailed to thousands across the country, edited by the current director, although much correspondence now takes place electronically.

During this decade, Jack Nelson traveled the country, meeting with seminarians and college students, enlisting new members for the Kirkridge fellowship, preaching in churches along the East Coast, in the Midwest, and even as far west as Fort Collins, Colorado. A recurring theme during these years in many of his sermons was a comparison of the "iron discipline" of the nations at war and that of the disciples of Christ.

Asking students at Penn State University on September 20, 1942, to "revolutionize the Church from within," Jack Nelson repeated his plea that these young people stay faithful to the Church because they were needed by "Negroes, relocated Japanese-Americans, and the world," adding that after the war they would be needed in "revolutionary careers" that would rebuild the nation and the Church.

Despite his hectic traveling and lecturing schedule, Jack Nelson still found time during this decade to edit *The Intercollegian* from 1943-1950. In 1946 he edited *We Have This Ministry*, and in the November 1, 1947 issue of *McCormick Speaking*, John Oliver Nelson (McCormick '33) had published an essay entitled "Ministers Beget Ministers." Because the audience of this publication was ministers (McCormick Theological is a seminary), he used this forum to propose his four-step plan for attracting a new generation of ministers:

1. Regard your own calling as merely an illustration of the way God calls every Christian to a life work;
2. Preach and talk the claims of Church vocations in sermons, youth groups, constant interviews with young people;
3. Keep in touch with youth;
4. Seek to live out unmistakably the joy and satisfaction of your calling.

With exuberance, Jack concludes that the slogan should be: "Considering a Church vocation? 'Ask the man who owns one.'"

In 1948 Jack published *The Church Is Young Again*, a book that, according to his diary, caused him no end of aggravation in editing. Throughout these years, Jack also continued to publish a monthly *Kirkridge Contour* and the "occasional" *Ridgeleaf.* Whether living in Philadelphia or New York, Kirkridge was never far from his heart or mind.

By 1948, John Oliver Nelson was beginning to wonder if he should consider a second ministerial position. Jack was offered the Heinz Chapel chaplaincy in Pittsburgh and $10,000 annually by another church through Dr. Buttrick. Upon great consideration and talking it over with his father, Jack chose to turn down both offers. As he writes in his diary for that year, his work was not yet done at the Federal Council of Churches, he was not fitted to administer, and both positions lacked proximity to Kirkridge.

JON's diary also gives indications of characteristics that would stay with him his entire life. Always a great communicator, Jack spent a Sunday in Amsterdam writing 160 postcards to family and friends.

An easy touch for friends down on their luck, Jack repeatedly lent money, and then discovered that his bank balance was overdrawn. Calling on his father to "bail him out" in February of that year, Jack also writes that John Evon Nelson on January 12 had cut off his $125 monthly allowance. Money problems would haunt Jack to the end of his life.

The Yale Years

1950-1960

In the fall of 1950, after ten years working with the Presbyterian Board of Christian Education and the Federal Council of Churches, John Oliver Nelson returned to his alma mater, Yale Divinity School, and began an academic career. His contacts with seminaries and colleges across the country surely enticed the Yale search committee, but as one of Jack's colleagues jokingly remarked in an interview, "Jack taught with his left hand."

The diaries Jack kept during the 1950s reveal a whirlwind of activity that often left him physically exhausted. As Professor of Christian Vocation and Director of Field Work, Jack taught a class in the Varieties of Ministry and eventually his was the only class in liturgy at Yale Divinity School.

While Jack was totally devoted to his students, those who taught with him remembered Jack as never being fully part of the Yale establishment; he was "vivacious, spontaneous, and not tied down by theological precision." This latter quality often put him at odds with the Divinity School administration and a diary entry from his first year at Yale records that the Dean's evaluation praised him for his field work, but cautioned that students felt he was sometimes preoccupied and unavailable. Jack writes, "In other words: Stay home and be Prof. Nelson. I must!"

But staying home and being Professor Nelson didn't come easily to Jack. His three resolutions for the 1952 new year were "to respect confidences, keep hands off people's lives, and accept few engagements!" Jack's history, however, shows he was rarely successful in the latter two resolutions.

Always active in the Fellowship of Reconciliation (eventually becoming Chair), Jack was constantly catching trains from New Haven to attend meetings in New York. In addition, he worked closely with the YMCA (an organization he had belonged to as a boy in Pittsburgh), taking over as National Secretary and as editor of their Association Press during this decade. In January of 1952, Jack was asked to become editor of the **Presbyterian Tribune**, and while he records a hearty "no!" in his diary, by February 14 he'd acquiesced, writing that the editorship was "dumped on me."

If these commitments were not enough to distract him from his decision to "be Prof. Nelson," Jack continued to direct retreats across the country and in Canada, and to preach on Sunday mornings at both local churches and at churches in New York, Connecticut, and Pennsylvania. Of course, Kirkridge was never far from his heart and mind. As part of his Kirkridge discipline, Jack traveled to his cell group in Rye, New York, monthly and to Kirkridge whenever he could get away.

The Fifties were years of building at Kirkridge. Weekends and holiday breaks would often find Jack and some of his friends or retreatants chopping trees, clearing brush, adding on a room to the Farmhouse, or learning to make bricks through trial and error.

9. Lodge (now called the Nelson Lodge) in 1952

10. Working on the Lodge – Summer of 1955:
Al Zadig, Ken Johnson, and Jack Lawe

11. Working on the Lodge – 1955

12. Work Retreat – June 20, 1956: Doug Sloan, John Cook

13., 14., 15. Building the Lodge – Summer of 1956

In the early days, all retreats added a component of manual labor, including domestic tasks of washing and drying dishes and sweeping floors. This shared commitment to sustaining and extending the Kirkridge community was a reflection of Jack's Iona experience, which was reinforced in the summer of 1955 when, at the invitation of George MacLeod, he went to Iona. Hoping to strengthen the bond he felt with Iona's founder, Jack worked on masonry at the abbey, peeled potatoes, and delivered buckets of fresh milk to the MacLeods.

When not working, praying, or attending worship services, Jack went to talks and discussions on the Christian life, the Church in the world, and the building of community—but he found few opportunities to "sit at the feet of the master." After finally setting up a meeting with Dr. MacLeod, Jack was angry when he "broke it rather bluntly." "Prima donna!" he writes. "He did invite me here."

Later Jack records one of his discussions with George MacLeod in which George advised him to consider marriage, even though Jack had encouraged his students to consider celibacy if they were not going to be directly involved in parish work.

At MacLeod's suggestion, Jack left Iona for Sigtuna, Sweden, on July 6 with 24 cents in his pocket. (SAS took a check for his flight.) In Sigtuna, he gave a lecture a day, most of them what he called his "canned" lectures given so often at American colleges, and these talks provided Jack with enough money to move on to the World Y Conference at Brussels. As a speaker at this conference, he received a $50 check, allowing him to take a train for Lyons and a visit with Brother Roger Schutz at the newly formed Taizé community. Promising Brother Roger $300 if he could come to Kirkridge, Jack left France for Germany and the site of the international FOR meeting. Jack was stunned by the ravages of war still evident in Köln and Düsseldorf after ten years.

As he traveled about with a German dictionary, he resolved to learn German when he returned home. The site of the international FOR meeting was the last stop on Jack's European journey, and here he spent time with his friend Douglas Steere of Pendle Hill. He wrote in his journal en route home, "The whole Iona experience a blessing and joy, making me rethink 1) celibacy, 2) liturgy, 3) making of community, 4) resolve to build."

Arriving home on August 1, Jack felt renewed in his dedication to his job and to the Kirkridge discipline. He vowed to keep his half hour of daily prayer again, and to make Kirkridge more a center for international peace by bringing races and religions together. Other promises were to continue to foster art at Kirkridge by getting a modern piece of art in each cell (bedroom) at Kirkridge, getting a "Steinway sooner or later," and sponsoring "real conferences on art."

In addition, Jack decided to get an architect to complete building plans for Kirkridge, to finish the book he had been struggling with, and to write FOR study materials. Finally, he wanted to "get clear my YDS [Yale Divinity School] motive and look conferees in the eye." In short, this European pilgrimage had provided new life to Jack's waning enthusiasm.

Financial problems never left Jack during the 1950s. Constantly helping out friends and students with loans he knew would never be repaid, he discovered his bank account was overdrawn on July 30, 1952, "the first time in 25 years." Except that it wasn't really the first time this had happened. It was the first time it had happened since his father's sudden death at age 72 on October 7, of the prior fall.

John Evon Nelson had supported Jack financially and emotionally all his life. In records for the years 1948, for example, we read that Jack's father donated $3,000 to Kirkridge; Jack donated $1,145.18, and 140 others had collectively given $921.50. His father's death, although shocking, did provide an inheritance of a few thousand dollars and many shares of Gulf stock--the valuable commodity that would build most of the buildings Jack dreamed of at Kirkridge. For the next ten years, Jack repeatedly paid overdue bills by cashing in his stocks at Gulf Oil.

When Jack and his friends began the Kirkridge experiment, the focus was primarily clergy evangelization and what they referred to as "movement for power in the Church." Like Jack, most of the early founders were Presbyterian, but by the 1950s the vision of Kirkridge had been enlarged to embrace many other denominations, even Catholics by the end of the decade. More women became active in the movement, donating money, observing the Kirkridge discipline, and coming for weekend retreats. In 1956, for example, the Board decided that women could be included in the summer seminary program.

The motto "Picket and Pray" reflects the strong commitment of these early members of Kirkridge to social action. In October of 1951, Kirkridge hosted an FOR Peace Training Unit, at no cost to the twenty men and women "who would carry out an agreed regimen of work, study, and worship along Kirkridge lines."

Many FOR meetings were held at Kirkridge during these years, as were YM/YWCA meetings. Jack's own commitment to the underserved was constant. In the summer of 1956, for example, while giving a retreat at Junaluska, North Carolina, he wrote in his journal: "Negroes here and accepted but not joyfully. We don't swim in lake because they can't."

Because these were still post-War years, Jack was committed to helping some of the displaced families pouring into the United States. The Emmerich Horvath family of Austria was the first to be brought to Kirkridge not only for a place to stay and work the land, but to acquire language skills so that they could eventually leave the mountain and obtain work in surrounding communities.

The Horvaths were followed by Andries and Ruth van der Bent and their family from Holland, who according to the 1958 Board minutes, were given authority in food purchasing, menu planning, kitchen supervision, and clerical work. Along with the Platts, the van der Bents became the caretakers of the Kirkridge property while Jack worked at Yale and traveled all over the country.

Rita M. Yeasted

Jack's vision of building a community of persons on the mountain was only partially realized. As the Platts aged and began to think of retiring and as the van der Bents' children grew and moved away, Jack realized that he needed a resident couple who would manage the property and lead retreats. His hopes were pinned on one of his former students, Hal Leiper and his wife Jane.

The son of Jack's friend, Henry Smith Leiper, his predecessor as Executive Secretary of the Federal Council of Churches, Hal was born in China. Henry and his wife had chosen to remain in China after the Revolution. Ordained a Presbyterian minister and a member of the Kirkridge Board, Hal seemed the perfect candidate for this task, and was already pivotal in the summer retreat program for the *Square Pegs* (seminarians Jack felt would never fit the mold of the average pastor).

Radicalized by his experience in China, Hal responded that he would take the summer position if Jack could endure his "communism." Jack assured him he could, and had high hopes that Hal, his wife, and their children would be the first family of Kirkridge. Jack could continue at Yale, knowing the work at Kirkridge would be in good hands. However, after experiencing the isolation of the mountain retreat and concerned about the family's unstable financial base, Jane Leiper decided that she did not want to rear the children there.

Hal had been an integral part of the early days of Kirkridge, and taking a post as YMCA chaplain at nearby Penn State in State College, Pennsylvania, allowed him to continue contact with Kirkridge. Unfortunately, this involvement was short-lived as Hal passed away at a young age. Jack still needed a resident couple to lead Kirkridge into the future.

Because Jack had always seen himself as a "five-year man," moving from one challenge to another after five years in a job, his 1955 diary shows him reflecting on whether he should leave Yale for another position. One of his most difficult tasks at Yale Divinity, according to Jack's notes, was the Admissions process. Hours and days of interviewing prospective candidates for the seminary was not the problem. Rather, Jack had a difficult time making the hard choices about who would be accepted and who would not, especially because he had recruited these young men in his travels throughout the country. To make matters worse, Jack was often the one who had to write the letters of rejection.

Colleagues of Jack's at Yale Divinity remembered that another onerous task for Jack was giving out scholarship money. Just as in his own life he often made bad choices when giving "loans" to people, Jack wanted to give scholarships to everyone who applied. Unfortunately, after exhausting all the departmental scholarship funds, Jack would find students in real need coming to his office presenting their plight. Friends remembered that he often took out his own checkbook and paid rent or tuition for students who really would have had to leave the university without help.

The years at Yale, though fulfilling on one hand, were also problematic for Jack Nelson. Always trying to be the scholar the administration expected him to be, he was haunted by deadlines for books and articles he could not get written, given his peripatetic lifestyle. Torn between his love of Kirkridge, his commitment to his students, his ministry to vocation awareness, and his many extracurricular jobs (such as giving retreats, editing numerous journals, and heading various organizations), Jack wrote often of his desire to rethink his academic life.

Eventually, however, he chose to stay at Yale for more than a decade. If for no other reason, his position at Yale provided a steady income and benefits. On February 27, 1954, he wrote: "Already I've paid $3,000 on new Lodge addition and [Bruce] Gelser's $3,500 for 1954 won't go far, I fear." In June of that same year, he noted in his diary: "K. bldg. cost Gelser $2,020, Stiles 8760, well 936, power 890, Brewer Plumbing 1260! Ach–and all for *me* to pay."

While it's clear from reading the journals that the years from 1950 to 1959 were important in Jack's ministerial career, it is also plain that worry about Kirkridge outpaced all other concerns; uncertainties filled his letters and diary entries for these years. Finding the mountain property and even gathering like-minded friends seemed easy compared with trying to keep the movement going during this decade.

Joe and Edith Platt remained the resident couple, but Jack felt the pressure of their impending retirement. In charge of correspondence and hospitality when guests arrived, the Platts interpreted Kirkridge to hundreds of retreatants and became the human face of Kirkridge. Interestingly, the Platts had come to Kirkridge via Jack's Quaker connections, especially with Douglas Steere.

Joe Platt, who had retired from YMCA work in China and Mongolia, was the model of Quaker patience, gentility, and deep reflective approach to life. In a letter dated June 23, 1952, John Casteel called this faithful Quaker couple "the living center of Kirkridge," and for many of the early guests, the Sunday afternoon tea and silence at Quiet Ways (the home they built on the property) became the most memorable experience of the weekend retreat.

While the Board met four times a year, and Jack came up to Kirkridge every chance he could, his absence from the day-to-day operation was proving problematic. An Advisory Committee was re-activated in 1955, providing Kirkridge with fresh ideas, new sources of income, and new contacts for retreatants and retreat leaders.

Many of these men and women had been inspired by Kirkridge a decade earlier, but distance and responsibilities made it impossible for them to serve on the Kirkridge Board. It's important to note that already in the early 1950s, Jack Nelson was a pioneer of "diversity"; women and persons of color were naturally and unselfconsciously included on the Board, even in the early 1950s.

But the real problem at Kirkridge was trying to meld the vision with the reality. The question of the Kirkridge discipline serves as one exemplar of this quandary. John Casteel, in a 1954 letter to the Platts, surfaced the dilemma with these revealing questions: "What are we trying to do at Kirkridge (as a place?); in Kirkridge as a movement?; and what are we severally as Kirkridgers trying to do in our own lives that can be pointed to as an attempt at least to carry out the intention?"

At this point in Kirkridge history, those who chose to be part of the "inner circle" promised to follow the discipline: to pray morning and evening, say grace at meals, tithe, read the daily Lectionary with its common Scriptural readings and hymns, work for the growth of a Christian cell group, make a personal retreat each month and an annual retreat at Kirkridge.

Each cell group member kept track of success or failure in this pattern of discipline through the quarterly report sheets. This record-keeping induced a great deal of discussion, prodded perhaps by guilt, and members began to wonder how effective adhering to this method actually was in achieving a dedicated life. Was there any assurance that this practice led to a deepening of the interior life? Was each of these demands of equal value? How did one decide?

John Oliver Nelson never did decide. Nor did the Platts nor the Board of Kirkridge, for the discipline was never "enforced" (nor could it be). Over time, fidelity to the discipline, while reaffirmed periodically, influenced fewer and fewer Kirkridgers.

Retreats that had been mainly for Square Pegs and seminarians expanded to include more and more church groups of lay men and women, all seeking something more than their local churches offered. And this new cohort brought another problem to the fore. Was the "work retreat" the *official* Kirkridge experience? How does one arrange a retreat for men who had been coming to Kirkridge for a decade or more while still providing a meaningful first-retreat experience for young ministers, seminarians, and lay persons interested in deepening their Christian life?

16. Lutheran Youth Leaders' Conference at Suomi
College, Hancock, Michigan on January 7, 1958: JON and
Dr. Marcus C. Ricke (American Lutheran Youth Director)

Evaluations show that often success eluded those leading the retreats. Board Minutes indicate that questions like those above permeated the decade, and in a letter to Joe and Edith Platt dated February 27, 1958, John Casteel bemoaned the fact that Kirkridge was not equipped to launch a very extensive program of lay training.

"We haven't leadership; we haven't the means for sustained effort; we haven't the facilities at Kirkridge; and we haven't the means for recruiting," he writes, adding "there's no point in our comparing ourselves, say, with Iona, which has the whole Church of Scotland as background–and MacLeod as foreground! We cannot really compare ourselves with the Church of the Saviour [in Washington, D.C.], where you have the daily living together of a committed group to make possible their long development of lay ministries."

Indeed, it was the Church of the Saviour that now became the model for Kirkridgers for what a commitment to "picket and pray" could really become in a local parish.

While the Platts, John Casteel, and other Board members worried about the future of Kirkridge, Jack Nelson began to contemplate his own future (as did others). In a letter dated April 10, 1953, Joseph Platt wrote to John Casteel:

> Jack himself might develop into the person who could carry out this dream. His almost total abstention from much unhurried time at Kirkridge for months, although he has generously given more money than ever before, his going to Iona, the evident restlessness and unsettlement of his life–may all perhaps be part of a great transformation. For this we pray.
>
> He has great qualities that, it seems to us, are not in harness or in focus but which could be used by God mightily through this movement.

Weary from the constant stress of travel, lectures, meetings, and a full-time job at Yale, Jack wrote in his diary as early as September 9, 1954: "Should I resign Kirkridge (and Oak Street [Project] and FOR)? Should!" That same day he flew to give a retreat at Five Oaks in Ontario, and on the 11th he met Jane Bone there.

In the back of the diary for that year, he wrote brief descriptions of persons he met at various conferences. In one entry, JON wrote: "Bone, Jane–Rev., Emmanuel Col.'50. DRE, and pastor, ...regular features, smart and only a little like Bess McBride [father's sister]. On 5 Oaks Staff now." Jane was an Associate Pastor at the Old High Park United Church in Toronto. During a sabbatical, she studied at Edinburgh University in Scotland, the same University Jack attended in years prior.

Now in his mid-40s, Jack questioned his life and his calling: "I'm falling apart!" he wrote in September of 1953. "Found bald spot developing this week. Receding gums bad and worsening." At a Y

Convention where he gave the closing address in the spring of 1954, he wrote, "A few good men around, most pretty middle-aged and weary." As was he.

The diaries are filled with reflections on loneliness during this period of his life. While he advocated that seminarians consider celibacy as a life choice, he also advised some to marry as "Loneliness does become a problem." Surrounded by students he counseled and helped financially, he still felt alone much of the time.

Jack's apartment was a haven for the distressed, the evicted, the needy, and often the annoying, but Jack offered hospitality to any seeking it, even though the experience of often getting to sleep long after midnight and getting up early for chapel at Yale Divinity left him exhausted. Having his brother Doug and his sister-in-law Jerry in New Haven helped somewhat. He was always welcome at their home, and when they announced that they were expecting a child at Christmas of 1956, Jack rejoiced with them.

But his own choice not to marry was taking its toll. On September 22, 1959, he wrote: "Every hour 4 new students and all a scramble and re-run sensation. Am I tired of all this, 10th yr.?" Jack had now doubled the years of his usual "five year plan." Looking forward to a sabbatical for the spring semester, he was ready for that transformation Joseph Platt saw coming.

From the first meeting with Jane McTaggert Bone at a 1954 seminar in Five Oaks, Ontario to the end of the decade, Jack occasionally mentioned her in his diary. There were phone calls, mentions of letters or postcards sent, a visit to Canada that included a dinner with Jane, and a struggle to know what to do about marriage. Few would doubt that the pressing need for a resident couple at Kirkridge, which was now reaching a crisis stage, influenced his decision, but for whatever reason, on April 19, 1959, the day before her 42nd birthday, he wrote in his diary: "Started letter to Jane Bone: This isn't exactly a love letter but I do want to underline.... The gal for me? See what she replies. She's to sail May 16 for U.K."

Eight days later, Jack (in Alfred J. Prufrock style) wrote: "Should I take sabbatical at Kirkridge 1960-1961? What about Jane Bone and plans to wed any time? Will I ever get a real job of MS [manuscript] writing done? Shall I let hair go white? Rewrite my will? Get a separate house?"

By August 27, some of those questions were answered: "Did buy car and house today! Car=1959 smoky gray Ford ranch wagon 8, $3,050 but 1,875 or so and my old green '55 Ford for close to ca. $1100. Got old conventional gear too, $189 less. Also to Clarence Bronson office to sign agreement for $17,500 on 94 Prospect St. Hi ho!" John Oliver Nelson, first-time homeowner, was about to have his life changed forever.

The end of this decade was marked far more by financial worries than plans for marriage. Paying bail for one of the many who wrote asking Jack for help, left him $500 poorer. By October 26, he admitted, "Bank balance $23.50!" On November 3, he wrote: "No sleep and worry all the time over 94 [address of his newly purchased home] and costs." Health worries also consumed him during this period: "I, having stopped rash on chest and creeping up to chin, now have sty." Yet the entry ends with admitting that he sent $37.50 for a friend's YMCA Vocation tests.

Three days later, Jack (never a good driver) ran through a stop sign and was hit by a '50 Chevy owned by a friend. "What a jumble," he wrote. "Probably $700 to $1,000." In typical Jack fashion, however, he rented a car for his *friend* after the wreckers towed the cars away and was driven home. The price of the house he had bought for $17,500 continued to climb. Repair and remodeling costs totaled nearly $4,000. As his father had done earlier, now his mother, Margaret, came to the rescue. That Christmas she gave him $3,000 and a loan for $25,000—with interest.

In the days before school began in 1960, Jack was doing much of the work in the house himself, with a few friends helping. He knocked out a partition on the third floor, refinished second-hand furniture, and did some painting. On May 13 he wrote: "Six painters swarm at 94," and less than a month later he decided to "redo the basement apartment, bath and all–a costly job."

In June he purchased a 1,000 gallon oil tank ($265 + labor), paid "$1,500 for downstairs carpet, $950 plumbers now (and $72 before!). Painter bill what? Ah me." The plumbing cost soared to $7,300 before their work was over, and while Jack commented on their exorbitant price, his obvious joy in having his own home shines through the pages of the diaries, as in the entry for April 28: "House building costs continue to mow me down: foolish for an old place like this? But fun!!"

What was not fun for JON in this spring semester was the loss of his dear friend, Hal Leiper on March 4, 1960. Hal passed away due to cancer, and was dearly missed. Jack tried to visit the Leipers when he could get away, and he attended the memorial service in Englewood on March 7. Later that day he wrote of Hal "real, lyrical, tenacious, impatient, child with secret." Now, however, he knew that his hopes were dashed for the Leipers as a resident couple at Kirkridge,and the search for a resident couple intensified.

Jack spent much of the summer of 1960 at Kirkridge, taking some time to visit his family at Chautauqua as usual. When not at Kirkridge, Jack worked on the house, worked in his office, attended his 30th reunion at Princeton.

17. Princeton Class of '30 reunion in 1960: Jerry Morgan, Charles Baton, JON (John Oliver Nelson)

18. Jack at his 30th Princeton reunion in 1960.

The summer also included a few college speaking engagements, Sunday services, and, in general, reflected on his life. On July 14, he wrote: "Me on romance journey now? Wonder if..." The next day he flew to Toronto for the weekend, met Jane for lunch at Tudor Hall ("a raffish place"), and had dinner with her at a Fifth Avenue restaurant. They talked of "marriage and family independence" until 12:15. On Saturday they went to a matinee of *Ben Hur*, drove to Pickfair and dinner in her old '49 Plymouth, then went to see *Suddenly Last Summer*, which Jack described as "gruesome, pathology."

After cake and orange juice at Jane's apartment and a brief kiss, he went back to the hotel, writing "I lonely? Need deep relation? Sacrifice too much by each? She 43, I 51. Slowly home and into troubled (Tennessee Williams) sleep." But two months later on September 18, he wrote: "Phoned Jane McTaggert Bone and said it is decided!! Call too casual and indirect? Bantering? Hope not."

He phoned his mother on October 23, promising that he'd visit on November 5–and added, "Jane: What size ring finger?" On November 8 he voted for Kennedy, took a train to New York and a plane to Toronto. He met Jane and ate at the Grenadier ("fine"). They went to Jane's "drab flat" and High Park United [Church of Canada] and talked of the ring and February 11, the date they had chosen for their marriage.

At news of the official engagement, Jack's mother sent Jane $3,000. Her attorney and family friend, Tommy Thompson, however, sent Jack a note in early January asking that he repay the $25,000 she had lent him "pronto." "How can I?" he wrote in the diary, having sent $1,000 in interest on the loan and $500 on the principal from the $3,000 gift she had given him for Christmas. Her generosity to Kirkridge endured. She sent $1,000 to Kirkridge in addition to the $1,000 she had given during the summer.

With a spring semester sabbatical promised, Jack hoped to marry with as little fanfare as possible, but on January 27 he entered the Yale Divinity School dining hall for lunch and was greeted with a banner, and a trumpet and trombone rendition of "Where, O Where, My Highland Laddies?"–during which Jack wrote he was "under the table."

Dean Liston Pope gave a speech and brought flowers, but while Jack was obviously pleased, he was also embarrassed. What he had tried to keep quiet was revealed when a reporter from Saskatchewan called the Divinity School for information about the Yale Professor that Jane Bone was engaged to marry.

As Jack had advocated celibacy for years, the shock and surprise of the announcement blended with good wishes for Yale's "most eligible bachelor." That everyone interviewed at Yale still remembered this event attests to its significance.

On Friday, February 10, Jack worked all morning finishing up a set of papers, grading a few internships, and typing two manuscripts, then he dashed off to his office at 1:00 to leave a $250 check for one of the needy students who had come to him for help. At 1:45 he picked up his brother Doug and at 2:45 they got Wenley. All three drove to Idlewild for a 4:30 flight to Toronto.

George Boyle met them at the airport, and at the rehearsal Jack, the consummate musician, "tooted Purcell's Trumpet Voluntary." Arthur Young invited the party to his home after the rehearsal, and "counseled" Jack before the party left on a snowy night at 1 a.m. Jack's notes about the wedding are brief, but he does write that he got a $1 gray tie (seemingly that morning), had breakfast at the Murrays, and that Doug drove the Volkswagen to pick up Jane for the 2 p.m. service at Iondale United Church, Scarborough.

Georgina Bone served as her sister's bridesmaid, with Wenley Nelson as best man. Rev. Arthur Young presided at the wedding, which Jack described as a "fine ceremony and reunion." Beverly Oaten of Five Oaks gave the "long and friendly" toast at the reception, and many from the party went with Jack and Jane to the airport, where they boarded a Swissair flight to Europe and a six-week honeymoon, "I addressing 50 cards. Both lay each on a 3-seat DC-8, what a day."

19. Jane Bone and JON's wedding on February 11, 1961 at Iondale United Church of Canada (UCC), Scarborough, Ontario

20. Jane Bone and her father, John Bone, on the day of her wedding

21. Doug, Wenley, Georgina, Jack, Jane, Mr. & Mrs. Bone, Margaret, May Young (Reverend's wife), Reverend Arthur Young, UCC

A Mountain of Possibilities

1961-1969

If the Sixties were a tumultuous time for America, neither John Oliver Nelson nor Kirkridge escaped the upheaval. Jack and Jane left for their honeymoon tour of Europe and the British Isles on February 11 and before they returned on March 21, they had traveled to Portugal, Spain, Italy, Beirut, Jerusalem, Switzerland, Denmark, Norway, Holland, and England, ending with a ferry ride to Iona with its "frigid bedroom and hot water bottles." Jack's brothers met the couple at Idlewild, and when they returned to New Haven, Connecticut Jack "carried Jane (stiff and laughing) over the threshold."

Marriage, however, never slowed Jack down. Two days after they returned, Jane and Jack drove to Canada to visit with Jane's family, then drove to Pittsburgh to visit with his mother, packing a trunk full of gifts for their home at 94 Prospect. During their first months home, Jack traveled to Dallas, St. Louis, and Ohio–and, of course, took Jane to Kirkridge for weekends, introducing her to the Board on April 7.

"Jane quiet and fits in well," he wrote in May. As Jack and Jane were in middle age, Jane wanted to begin a family as soon as possible. That hope was dashed when each month passed without a pregnancy, and, as Jack wrote in his diary, "Do I *want* a child?" Whatever his reservations, the couple were ready to consider artificial insemination, when in September of 1961 Jane and Jack were told to stop trying because of her previous bout with cancer. "Gloom here," he noted.

A week after they returned from the annual Presbyterian retreat, however, Jane got a second opinion from her doctor in Canada: "Five years, no cancer," Jack wrote. "Go ahead to procreate, so thermometer each a.m."

Besides Jane's great desire to have a child, this first year of marriage had other stresses. Jack was haunted by Kirkridge's need for a full-time couple to direct the activities there. After a Board meeting in October, Jack wrote that while a new booklet was needed for the 20th anniversary of Kirkridge, "still decision depends on going to K. for good." Jack continued to hold his position at Yale not only for a steady income and benefits, but because he didn't know if the move would be best for Kirkridge or for Jane.

And still the travels continued: a retreat at Davidson College in North Carolina in October and at Easton's Lafayette College in November. On December 15 he returned to his alma mater, Princeton, writing in his journal: "Triangle show *tour de force*! Ah, nostalgia!" On Christmas Eve he and Jane traveled to Pittsburgh to spend the holiday with his family.

The new year brought Jack and Jane new challenges. Jane continued to give retreats, join New Haven social action groups, and study United States history. On March 12 she held a British tea for 16, complete with a Union Jack and a rendition of "God Save the Queen." That same day, someone suggested Jack as dean of the Divinity School, a position he neither wanted nor felt qualified for.

And still Jane hoped for a child to complete the family. In March the question of adoption rose, and as a trial run, the couple took in a 14-year old named Rick, who needed a stable home. In May Jack wrote that he liked Rick, that he'd taken him to Lovell School and had his bike repaired.

Yet his diary for that year also reflects Jack's ambivalence about fatherhood. "Rick still a quandary," he wrote a few months after the boy came to live with them, and the ambivalence must have gone both ways. Rick's comment that "Dad looks distinguished even at

Mc Donald's" was important enough to Jack that he copied the words in his diary for July 25. JON and the newest member of the Nelson family made a real attempt to bond: "If you push me too much I'll let you know," Rick told Jack (who noted it in his diary).

The three traveled to Nantucket that summer and to Chautauqua, which Rick loved. While Rick made new friends at Hagen summer camp, Jane and Jack kept up their hectic schedule of talks and retreats in Canada, Washington, D.C., Cape May, New Jersey, and Nashville for the NaCoMe meeting (a Presbyterian summer camp named for the three Presbyteries of that time: Nashville, Columbia, and Memphis), and the AFSC (American Friends Service Committee) Conference at Sunnybrook, Pennsylvania. Then both returned to Kirkridge for a spiritual healing retreat. Before the summer was over, plans for the Leiper Room at the Lodge were complete.

With $1,200 on hand the work began that month, but Jack noted that he missed seeing Rick's three counselors at 94 Prospect Street, as once again he was at Kirkridge trying to direct activities, while not living there.

Married for a year and a half, and now "father" to a teen-ager, Jack began another fall semester at Yale. The school year got off to a rocky start. After Father Gerald Sloyan of Catholic University spoke on liturgical reform, and following a sharp disagreement with the worship panel, Jack wrote in his diary that the faculty were "liturgically illiterate."

22. Nelson family photo: Jack, Jane, and Rick

What had always been a frenetic schedule for Jack now included trying to fit in Jane's scheduled retreats and conferences, where she was a leading figure, further compounded by caring for a son whose academic progress never satisfied Jack. In November he attended the PTA meeting at Tukelan and decided that private tutors might help Rick to improve his grades and attitude towards school.

That same month he turned down the chairmanship of the Council of Churches World Mission Committee, but wondered if he should have considered another position as chair offered him by the national office. In a November 27 journal entry Jack wrote, "Should I have considered the CDE job for myself? Commute to NY, etc.? Not popular at YDS and indeed not centrally interested in academic stuff." Certainly, Jack's failure to publish and his extra-curricular travel did make him a less than stellar colleague at YDS, but his gift for representing the university at other academic campuses and his availability to students were valued contributions, as attested to by his colleagues in interviews. The indecision about taking over as director at Kirkridge, however, remained.

The home he, Jane, and Rick shared at 94 Prospect Street was seldom without other guests, including the occasional friend of Rick's, who, like him, needed a safe home. As friend to the friendless for most of his life, the down-and-out continued to call on Jack, asking for money, a place to stay until they could get back on their feet, or simply a place to stay. This situation could not have been easy for Jane. On New Year's Day, one of the guests invited for dinner was supposed to be back at the VA Hospital by 9 p.m. Instead, he had five drinks, walked off with Rick's knife, and returned wielding a knife and frightening the rest of the guests. Jack called the police, but not before the women present were screaming in fear.

As was his usual wont during this season, an unfazed Jack ended the evening by working on Christmas cards, a task he called "heartsome work," that would remain one of the great joys of his life. His entry for January 2 reads: "All my cards late, late, almost for Russian Christmas Jan. 7, partly because our adopting 15-year-old Richard upsets all domestic timetables!"

Safely back in the VA Hospital, Jack's friend wrote that he hated him, yet by February 9, he was back at the Nelson table with other friends, and Jack could report that most of the manuscript was completed for *Vocation and Protestant Church Occupations*, although it was due February 1.

Two themes persist in Jack's diaries for the early years of this decade: a continuing dissatisfaction with the Vietnam War and, interestingly, with the YMCA's growing emphasis on what Jack called "non-Christian programs," especially behind the Iron Curtain. His protests about both themes brought new friends and lost him old ones. Jack's pacifist roots were deep; he was one of the founding members of the Fellowship of Reconciliation (FOR) and a long-time member of the Peace Fellowship of the Presbyterian National Office, the Christian Peace Mission, and various other organizations devoted to peace and justice. Just as the war became a divisive issue across America, it affected the lives of Jack and Jane throughout the Sixties and into the Seventies.

Jack began to take part in anti-war debates on the Yale campus, and during one of his talks at a Methodist church, the inviting minister, an ex-military chaplain, became so angry with Jack that he gave him only $25 for the talk, considerably less than he had expected. Worries about paying bills and being out of cash fill the pages of his diaries during these first years of marriage, and thus he hesitated to give up the security of a full-time position at Yale.

What's more, some of the problems that plagued Jack before his marriage persisted during it. A few men continued to come to him for loans, bail, and advice, although they seldom took the good advice he offered. He bought bus tickets and second-hand cars for more than one friend to enable him to get to a job or school.

Jack would usually pay when the cars were in accidents, pick up the cost of insurance, and even cover bad checks of one friend, who seemed to have been in and out of his life for twenty years. One man during this period took Jack's credit card to pay for gas during a trip, running up numerous other charges in the interim. Jack not only never prosecuted these hangers-on, but always hoped that if he gave them one more chance, they might turn their lives around. It was a costly, if Christ-like, mercy.

On May 27, 1963, two weeks after Jack's 54th birthday, the final adoption papers were signed for Richard Campbell Dodds Nelson before Probate Judge Rescitelli, in Hamden, Connecticut. The new family celebrated with milkshakes at McDonald's at 5:00 that evening.

The next day Jane was off to Saskatoon for her parents' golden wedding anniversary celebration and Jack once again sold Gulf shares to help pay the bills. By late August, he was writing again about whether he should stay at Yale or resign. "God's will vs. my course?" he queried on September 20, now beginning what would become his last semester on the Yale faculty.

At the November Board meeting at Kirkridge, the final decision was made. The Board would provide $6,200 for the Nelsons and $4,200 for Lawrence Telford (Larry) Young, a 1962 YDS graduate, as program director, the latter having spent a year at Iona in preparation for the post. On November 6 Jack wrote his letter of resignation to the Yale Divinity School committee on faculty.

Another Christmas passed, with the usual trip to Pittsburgh and complaints about late card sending, but on January 7 he wrote, "Still mixed thoughts about leaving." Less than two weeks later, however, he received word that the Platts wanted to retire and move to Media as soon as possible, so there was no turning back. Sir George MacLeod's visit in early December affirmed Jack's decision, and his approval helped Jack to begin looking forward instead of back.

With Rick's impending high school graduation, it seemed clear that Jack's dream of a Nelson education for him wasn't going to materialize. When the guidance counselor suggested that Jack and Jane allow him to go to the Army, get married, and not attempt college, Jack was stunned, especially since his anti-war protesting had been so pronounced, but trying to be good parents, they acquiesced.

On February 13 Jack wrote in his diary that perhaps they should adopt a girl, but that hope never materialized either. It was 1964, and the conflict of making such momentous decisions took its toll on Jack's health. On March 6 he wrote, "Wretched, I am. Sacrum creaks, tooth thermally aches, all tired and spent!"

Yet he left for a retreat at Holy Cross the next morning, writing on the 9th: "On road all day—sick and weary, I sleep." Neuralgia in his right cheek and recurring sciatica seemed to be the main culprits, but the small family still traveled to Pittsburgh for Easter, where Jack found his mother "in past week way down, ... dreamed of her funeral and who there." A Van Cliburn concert over the weekend cheered him, but he found his mother bad company, and came home worried about her frailty and "spells."

On April 10, Jack wrote in his diary a list of reasons for making the decision to go to Kirkridge and leave Yale; among them, the crisis of the Platts wanting to leave as soon as possible, the dream of bringing clergy and laity together not apart, time to write, and the past ten years of "just scholastic corollaries of big Barth rebellion" at Yale. The move would also give Jack the chance to explore "liturgy and arts vs. theology," and, he added, "14 yrs. to go [before retirement] and must get cracking."

Reality set in, however, with the last comment: "half the salary, twice the work!" On the 17th Jack and Jane went to the Kirkridge Board meeting, where Joseph Platt formally resigned. On Jane's 47th birthday, April 20, the news release of their going to Kirkridge (which Jack wrote) was released; it appeared on the front page of the *New Haven Register* on April 27.

On May 9 the Leiper Room was formally dedicated, and a farewell party was held for the Platts, who had incalculable influence on early Kirkridgers and on Jack's passion: a united movement for power in the Church. The Quaker silence that marked every early gathering at Kirkridge came about because of the Platts' own commitment to it. The "tea and symphony" gatherings at their home, Quiet Ways, ended most weekend retreats and are among the best memories of early Kirkridgers. As the first resident couple at Kirkridge for nearly twenty years, the Platts played an essential role in Jack's story and that of Kirkridge.

The bittersweet move from New Haven, Connecticut, to the Poconos in Pennsylvania took a toll not only on Jack but on Jane and Rick as well. Jane's May 14 birthday card to Jack for this year indicates her deep love for him, an appreciation for his work, and demonstrates her sense of humor. The card reads: "I wanted to send a birthday candle that was just right for you.... [inside] so here's one that burns at both ends!" Her handwritten message reads: "Beloved,

How you make yours 'last the night' and yet 'give a lovely light' is a mystery to me and to others. At whatever end–long may it burn! My best love to you–Jane."

The faculty held a farewell party for the couple on May 22, which Jack described as "sad." Rick, now driving, sped to Kirkridge with plants and books, and got a speeding ticket, a fate that befell Jack numerous times. On the 23rd Jack and Rick loaded their belongings for another trip to Kirkridge.

A week later they celebrated Rick's 17th birthday with a noon party at which he received "a razor, a lighter, and two clocks!" When Jack had to forgo his annual trip to the Princeton Crusaders, he wrote that the phone response was "rather curt," but a couple was coming to view their New Haven home, which they hoped to rent for $175 a month, so the future held some promise.

In the summer of 1964, June marked a historical month of transition for JON. Those who knew Jack personally or listened to the audiotapes he recorded shortly before his death know he took great pride in relating how a Roman Catholic Archbishop Roberts, S.J., of India held the first Catholic Mass at Kirkridge on June 12 at 7:30 in the evening. Jack never tired of reiterating the historical importance of this event, to illustrate the ecumenical nature of Kirkridge just twenty years after its founding.

Yet JON's diary shares his initial reflections of the event: "lots of kissing of table, etc., trop [too many] saints named! But good farewells." Kirkridge, like Iona, would be a home for all Christians-- even the "RCs" with their proliferation of saints. In fact, the RCs were meeting that weekend at Kirkridge to discuss civil rights.

June was a time of many Nelson farewells. Jack and Jane had last meetings with Yale Hope, a rescue mission for men founded by William W. Borden early in the 20th century, and especially dear to Jane, who also was involved with Wider City Friends and the Connecticut Council of Church Women. Rick would leave friends and easy access to teen-aged city activities. And Jack would leave a coveted profession and national contacts at Yale,. He kept almost all of his other commitments in New York City and across the country. No quick train ride into the city would exist for any of them, however, and travel would become more complicated as the years passed, especially in winter.

On June 25 the movers brought the rest of the furniture to Kirkridge, with only Jane's cane back chair damaged. A retreat on vocational choice in late July attracted only "8 but they paid. Best of all." The summer brought the annual vacation to Chautauqua and a much relieved decision by Rick to attend a junior college instead of joining the service. A long talk with Jack's mother during this vacation concerned the destiny of the family home in Pittsburgh. Would it be given to Pittsburgh Theological or Fred Rogers, a family friend, Presbyterian minister, associated with Pittsburgh Theological, and later host of the television show *Mister Rogers' Neighborhood*?

Since no one in the family wanted to live there, this was not a small consideration for such a beautiful home. In September Jane and Jack learned first-hand how complicated going to New York would now be. They took a bus into the city to attend the Kirov Ballet, but had to leave before it was ended in order to catch the bus home.

As executor of his mother's will, Jack flew to Pittsburgh that month to speak with lawyers. His mother at 84 had suffered a small stroke but was still considered a "marvel" of good health. Before the month was over, however, Rick shocked Jack and Jane, informing them that he would like to enlist for military service.

On October 14 he took a bus for Easton to join the paratroopers. Jack's objection to the Vietnam War would only grow as the years passed, but his concern for Rick's safety grew as well. A November stay at the Trappist Monastery in Kentucky for a peace meeting with the Berrigan brothers, Thomas Merton, John Grady, James Forest, and Tom Cornell was one of many meetings that increased as the war progressed. Since peacemaking has been part of Kirkridge since its inception, Jack's choice of gray stock for his 1964 Christmas cards may have reflected his gloom.

The first full year as the resident couple at Kirkridge brought more trials. JON's commitments to preaching, giving talks, and recruiting seminarians for the Square Peg meetings, plus planning for the future–and paying the bills–left little time for the writing he had hoped to do, although he did write on New Year's Day that his goal was to write a "liturgy a day" for a Kirkridge Daily Liturgy, similar to the Iona Worship Book. Jane fell on the ice in January and landed in the hospital with a knee injury. Two lambs were lost, and Jack complained of sleeping poorly.

Aunt Marnie died in February, two weeks after Jack went to Fort Jackson to visit Rick, who was "a fine sight." With spring there were more talks to give at Penn State University in State College, a Western State YMCA retreat, a Pingry School of Religion Conference in Chattanooga, several Buck Hill retreats and talks, and a talk at the Missionary Orientation Center at Stony Point, New York.

At Easter he and Jane drove to Pittsburgh to be with his mother, who seemed to be "failing rapidly," and also visited with Aunts Massa and Bessie. Three weeks later, Jack took a late train to Pittsburgh for the Y National Board conference and drove out to visit his mother, finding her "rickety."

Now Jack had the opportunity to see his vision for Kirkridge come to life, and in the early days, he planned art-focused events, what were called "occasions." The July 1965 occasion drew only a small number of participants, however. The promotion of good liturgy, another of Jack's passions, drew him to St. John's Abbey Spiritual Life Institute in August, where "all the big RC names on liturgy" were gathered: Barnabas Ahern, Godfrey Dieckmann, OSB, Bernard Häring, Jean Leclercq, OSB, plus Church of the Saviour's Gordon Cosby, and Bob Raines of Germantown, who would one day succeed Jack as Kirkridge director. Jack complained of having no shower ("just Arrid®") there, but he also "spoke on Kirkridge, wrote lots of cards, saw lots of colorful art in Minnesota, and got little sleep.

A "radiant" Jane met him at the JFK airport (renamed a month after Kennedy's assassination). The day after Jack returned, Rick wrote that he would be in Hawaii for three months' machine-gun training for Vietnam. The hated war had finally come home.

From the time he purchased the property that would become Kirkridge, one of Jack's unrequited dreams was to build a church on the mountaintop. Likely inspired by the abbey on Iona, this would give him a chance to fulfill his desire to wed good art and good architecture in church design. In September of his first year at Krikridge Jack began to discuss building an A-frame chapel.

With little cash for this project, the Board refused the idea in favor of more immediate needs. In fact, minutes of the Kirkridge Board for September 13-14, 1964, show that Jack "outlined a proposal to build a worship center on the knoll between the Farmhouse, Darwood and Upper House where the daily office of the Kirkridge community would be celebrated. It would have great value as a symbol of unity relating the life and work going on in and the units around it as a total act of worship." The concepts of "daily office" (Jack's Daily Liturgy) and a Kirkridge "community" emphasize Jack's dream of building an American Iona, so similar is the relationship, but Board member Rustum Roy urged Jack to keep in mind "our concern that the church is in the world."

March 29, 1959 at Darwood, Kirkridge, Bangor, Pa.
Edith Platt, Irma + Fritz vanderbent, George Buciarski, JONelson, Ans vanderBent, Joseph Platt,
Pete Ingalls, (back of heads:) Ruth vanderBent, (profile) Betty Ingalls

23. Darwood (early Nelson residence) at Kirkridge March 29,
1959. In the circle (left to right): Edith Platt, Irme and Fritz
van der Bent, George Buciarski, JON, Ans van der Bent,
Joseph Platt, Pete Ingalls (back of heads in foreground)

Because no resident community yet existed on the mountain,
the Board reviewed the decisions made at the Bishop John A.T.
Robinson retreat concerning the "Covenanter" plan. This plan, first
proposed by Joseph Platt in 1958, advocated the formation of five
East Coast geographical groupings, "both to support Kirkridgers
in their endeavors and to undergird the Kirkridge program." Five
areas and conveners were chosen: New York City-New Jersey,
Philadelphia, Boston, Rochester, and Lehigh Valley. If Jack could not

have his resident community, these 35 Covenanters, which he called Kirkridge's "immediate family," would be the next best thing.

In a letter to the 35 Covenanters dated March 10, 1965, Jack writes, "Granted, that the original Scots 'covenanters' were a sturdy outfit who clung nobly to a pact (Church-and-State) which history had long since passed by: our 'Covenanters,' it's to be hoped, may somehow get ahead of the history of the time–which isn't doing too well in any case."

This newly formed group of Kirkridge was sent a copy of Henry Clark's ***The Christian Case Against Poverty*** free of charge, with the request that each person send reactions or set some time by for discussions sometime within the next months. "Covenanters are the movement [for power in the Church]," Jack concludes, "and the strength and grace of your taking part are of the essence if Kirkridge is to make its witness." By June the number of Covenanters reached 50.

Board member Reverend Gerald Jud's September retreat, using Harvey Cox's newly published ***Secular City*** as a starting point, was a great success. However, Jack commented in his diary that the retreat was "not too workish, but then most occasions minimum on labor these days," work being a component of all early Kirkridge retreats. Kirkridge was about to change in other ways.

Always looking at areas and needs not met by the institutional church, Jack centered his concerns more and more on youth, whom he felt were lost to the Church and their parents. No longer in direct contact with the students at Yale Divinity, Jack missed the interaction. The idea of building a school at Kirkridge seems to have been there from the beginning. Jack had explored folk schools in Sweden a decade before, and he questions in diary entries whether a new type of Christian education, not Sunday school, but an integrated curriculum that combined academics with service, might be feasible. Since Larry Young asked to be relieved of his job as program director, Jack and Jane had a new opportunity to fashion Kirkridge into their image.

Jack's constant traveling was questioned by the Board, who suggested that perhaps he should stay closer to home. At the same time, he was the ambassador for Kirkridge and its programs, and staying on the mountain and waiting for people to come did not seem a viable option.

What Jack most wanted for Kirkridge was the formation of a resident community of committed Christians under discipline. This model was directly patterned after the Iona Community, and one familiar to those early Kirkridgers who twenty years earlier meticulously kept the Kirkridge devotional discipline and reported their spiritual progress. That, and a chapel on the mountaintop.

By year's end, Jack and Jane reluctantly had to find a new home for their beloved Mayme Sullivan. She was moved to Gracedale the weekend of Thanksgiving when Square Pegs from eleven different schools arrived at Kirkridge. Jack wrote on December 3 that she was unhappy there, as she couldn't have her dog Blackie, but there was not a good alternative, given her health problems.

Because Rick was expecting a leave over the holidays, Jack and Jane decided to hold off on a planned trip. When they heard that Rick would spend the leave with a friend, they decided to visit Jack's mother in Pittsburgh for Christmas, and then travel to San Francisco and Mexico.

January/66 John and Jane Nelson, Acapulco, Mexico

24.-25. Jack and Jane Nelson vacationing in Acapulco, Mexico aboard SS Fiesta on January 15, 1966

26. JON and Jane at Hotel El Presidente, Acapulco on January 18, 1966 with Sidney Francis Smith III

The trip through the Southwest and Mexico was more than a vacation. Jack began looking at schools, the Verde Valley School in Phoenix for one. In Mexico, where Jane became very ill, the two enjoyed the Ballet Folklorica and Mexican art. They drove from Mexico City to Acapulco, relaxed in the sun, and flew back to Newark on January 20 with "lots of slides."

In his journal entry for the day, Jack wrote of how grateful to God he was for the trip, although he was bothered by the contrast between rich and poor that they found there. "How short the time and vital the one job at K!" he wrote, but he failed to define what he saw as the "one job." New year's activities would give little hint of Jack's main focus.

Nine days after they returned from Mexico, Jack was asked to run for the Pennsylvania Congress against a candidate named Rooney on an anti-Vietnam stance. "Scares me stiff!" he wrote. "March through May campaign. I dilettante, really keen on anti-LBJ?" He never seriously considered this run, but that he would be asked by others to run gives some indication of his wide recognition as a peace activist.

At the September 1966 Board meeting the possibilities for developing a Lehigh Valley industrial mission were discussed. Jack's concern for workers and workers' rights was lifelong. His association with Dorothy Day and the Catholic Worker Movement began in the 40s, and his introduction to industrial missions began in Scotland, for they were prominent during his study there. This movement, which attempted to "build bridges" connecting industry, the Church, and society, developed missions in many of the Northeastern cities Jack visited.

When looking for the greatest contribution Kirkridge could make to the Church and in the world, the Board felt compelled to consider an industrial mission. Gerald Jud proposed at this meeting that Kirkridge become an "initiator of ministries," affirming that because they "are in a time of turning and revolution in the church, .

. . engagement in industrial mission is consistent with the Kirkridge spirit and style."

In the words of the Board minutes, "in a time when the residential congregation is under fire because its deeds do not match its words, Kirkridge also must act on its incarnational theology; it must become involved in the world-context in which it is set." Jud added that "in the future the most significant theological insights will come from those places where reflection and action go on together; exciting theology comes from battle fronts rather than from ivory towers."

Scott Paradise, formerly on the Detroit Industrial Mission staff but then the director of the Boston Industrial Mission, spoke at length to the Board about his experience with this movement, warning the members that progress is very slow, and long-term investment of personnel and money is required.

Gunther Sahling also spoke to the Board from the point of view of a union member, reminding the members present that an industrial mission "explores the needs of a Christian in today's industrial society and then equips him to live in this society." While Kirkridge never officially became an industrial mission, its mission and programs through the years certainly focused on these important issues.

Berthi van der Bent, who had known Jack for many years, described him as "the rich young man with black-rimmed finger nails wherever he went . . . whether visiting the 'lads' in prison or teaching at Yale or leading retreats. These tiny black lines in otherwise clean and neat hands," she recalled, "were a dead giveaway of solidarity at once for those who didn't 'have,'" that Jack's identification with *them* "was instant without a word spoken."

The winter months saw great activity at Kirkridge. The Farmhouse living room was expanded, with the addition of new doors. The Folly, a small dwelling next to the Lodge, was "being manicured for real living." The van der Bents, whose ceramic Celtic crosses would become a Kirkridge symbol–even though Ruth van der Bent tried to assure Jack that crosses weren't needed because Christ was

Risen—nonetheless asked for a new kiln fuse board and a headroom for ceramics in the cellar. And two lambs were born to the "stray Cheviot ewe."

The January 9, 1967 Board meeting proposed a colloquy in the area of theology and the arts, featuring W.H. Auden and Arthur Miller, and while this was never held, it does offer insight into Jack's continuing focus on bringing the arts into discussions of theology. By February, Jack was faced with a multiplicity of directions for Kirkridge.

Should Kirkridge build a youth hostel, as the AYH (American Youth Hostels) now wanted, or should Jane Leiper be brought in to work with youth groups? Should *Cimade*-type groups be trained here by a resident couple, in the manner of this French association founded to aid displaced persons in Europe?

Should Kirkridge establish a secondary school with an organizer hired for one year to gather data and approach foundations? Could Kirkridge build a real lay academy or folk school? Could a rehabilitation center for clergy be set up? And finally, "Should I spend (give) $100,000 to do all this?" Jack's inheritance *would* fund many of these projects–and many more in the years to come.

A week after the Kirkridge Board meeting that February, Jane, 48, suffered a miscarriage, ending a three-month pregnancy. Jack described her as "miserable" over the loss. Although her sister-in-law recalled knowing of more than one miscarriage during the first years of marriage, JON's diaries do not mention another one after this date. On the 11th Jack took Jane to New York City to celebrate their fifth wedding anniversary. They both looked forward to their second spring and better weather on the mountain.

At the March Board meeting, members spent considerable time discussing the main thrusts of Kirkridge for the immediate future. The Board thought that perhaps the industrial mission would satisfy the obligation to bring the world and the Church together. Jack presented a mission stemming from his personal vocation at Kirkridge:

- Research and deepening in the theology of devotion (how one prays in the modern day), with experimental thrusts in liturgy;
- Renewal of theological education, providing a "loyal opposition" which confronts seminary leaders with new frontiers;
- Reappraisal of youth and student ministries toward preparing for the church of the future;
- Psychological and spiritual rehabilitation of ministers (and laymen);
- Provision of a place–an esthetic visual symbol marked by contemporaneity, simplicity, drama.

In light of this discussion, the Board decided to re-examine Kirkridge's charter, which emphasized clergy renewal. All agreed to work on a simplified version of the charter before year's end.

With Rick in Qui N Hou, Vietnam (scheduled for an August 31 return), and Jack traveling all over the East Coast by car, train, and plane, Jane held down the fort at Kirkridge. Requests for money continued to besiege Jack: $4,000 for a used car lot (turned down), $50 for alimony, $24 bus fare, upkeep costs on seven cars, almost all in need of constant repair.

Monthly payments on a large loan made in New Haven continued to stretch the budget–as did the repeated fines Jack incurred for speeding offenses. Jack continued his association with the Evangelism Division of the National Council of Churches, the FOR, the Y and Association Press in New York, plus his Church Peace Mission involvement.

He visited Mount Saviour Monastery in late March to speak about Kirkridge during a Lenten talk, commenting on their "perfect chanting." On April 2 he purchased ten $20 Cheviot-Marino ewe lambs from McElyea–Southdowns–but "they have ticks, alas." The sheep, which had been a part of Kirkridge from the Platts' time there, kept the grass down, with the hope that they might also one day provide food for the retreatants.

Jack bought a new "sauterne gold Ford" on Good Friday, trading in the Fairlane before leaving for his mother's for Easter. He bought Jane a new suit and coat in Harrisburg for Easter Sunday, and the couple found Mrs. Nelson in relatively good health. They attended a concert on Saturday night after flower shopping. Easter Sunday included the obligatory visit to his aunts Bess and Massa. His mother and aunts all hoped to come to Kirkridge on May 16, and Jack purchased the plane tickets for them on the 28th of April.

Earlier that month, Jack attended an all-day FOR meeting on the 20th. Although he tried to focus his energies on Kirkridge, he accepted the offer of renewed chairmanship with a heavy heart. In his diary, he reflects upon the mounting commitments and inner struggle he faced with being pulled in too many directions. A trip to Washington, D.C., a stopover to visit with his mother, while speaking at a suburban Pittsburgh church, and he was back at Kirkridge for a retreat that was mercifully called off for lack of attendance, giving him time to do "prep school at K stuff."

When the Board met on May 7, Keith Irwin was hired to work full-time at Kirkridge, replacing Larry Young. Three new task forces were formed to investigate the foundation of a halfway house, prep school, and youth hostel.

Jack's 55th birthday was spent, as usual, on the road, although he notes that Jane was up to see him off for Nyack, NY, where he spoke to a group of Methodists on "Twentieth-Century Churches." In July he and Jane spent a restful week at Chautauqua, and two weeks after their return, they spoke to Children's Aid about adopting another child. "Dunno," Jack wrote in his diary for July 15.

Two days later, with the airlines on strike, he drove to Earlham College in Richmond, Indiana, where he taught theology to Quaker students until the 21st, hopping a bus to Chicago, where he spent the night before taking another bus to New York City to give a series of talks and classes at Union Theological Seminary until August 5.

Taking a bus to Washington, D.C., Philadelphia, and finally Stroudsburg, Jack arrived home at 12:15 a.m. "Read mail till 2 a.m., overjoyed to see Jane again and be in my own bed after three weeks!" he wrote, and he stayed home for a week–except for a trip to Buck Hill Falls, Lancaster County, with Jane, and then while she preached in Bangor on August 14, he was off to D.C. for a week at Wesley Theological Seminary and NTL (National Training Laboratories) training in leading T-Groups.

The experience of self-reflection and group interaction was both painful and helpful for Jack, who also led a chapel service each morning for participants who wanted to attend. He found some participants disliked him, criticized him for not being engaged enough, and found him too intellectual, too "Ivy League."

On the other hand, Jack was supported by others in the group, and was complimented for the fine worship services and Michel Quoist prayers. He left for Kirkridge satisfied that the experience had been a "very good" one. He agreed to come back the following August for $650 plus travel expenses.

The Board at their August meeting decided to discontinue the use of the word "Covenanters," Jane explaining that upon consideration, use of the term had found favor neither with those so designated nor the others who were not. On August 24 Jack registered as a Democrat for the first time. By the time he left for Pendle Hill on September 7 for the Spiritual Life Institute, bulldozing to construct a new center for recovering alcoholics had begun.

The School Task Force met on September 17, reporting that the school would eventually house 30 boys and 30 girls, with the hope of beginning in September of 1967. Rick came home on September 22, matured, silent, thin, tatooed, and bearing medals. Jack and Jane rejoiced at his safe return. But JON seldom stayed at Kirkridge for long.

Wofford College in Spartanburg, SC, hosted Jack for a Young Life meeting, and then he was back to preach at a Bangor Methodist

Sunday service. He drove to Williamsport, Pennsylvania on October 10 where he preached at Lycoming College. An FOR meeting on October 18 took him to New York City, and two days later he called his mother, writing that she was fine and planning a trip to the Westminster Symphony in New Wilmington, Pennsylvania.

On Sunday the 23rd Jack was off to Akron, Pennsylvania, for a meeting of "progressive Mennonites" on renewal, rushing home for a 3 p.m. Board meeting Monday at Kirkridge. At 11:30 that night, however, he received a call from Dr. Haber at West Penn Hospital, informing Jack that his mother was admitted and was critically ill. At 12:30 a.m. October 24, 1966 Margaret Dodds Nelson, 86, died of a ruptured aneurism after attending the symphony performance on Saturday evening, church on Sunday and dinner with the Thompsons, the family attorney.

27. Jack and his mother Margaret on a cruise, December. 20, 1957

Jack called Doug and Wenley "pronto," and he and Jane left for Pittsburgh the following morning. Jack had to release his mother's body and make funeral arrangements with Samson Funeral Home, while waiting for his brothers and sister Peggy, who had to fly in from Los Angeles.

Rick flew in for the funeral, and Jack picked him up at the airport. Doug and Tom Thompson were executors of the estate, and at the reading of the will Jack discovered that his mother had left $30,000 to Kirkridge, the Chautauqua home to Peggy, the house to Pittsburgh Theological Seminary, and a quarter of the estate to each of the four siblings. Eugene Ormandy was among those who sent flowers, as Mrs. Nelson, a pianist herself, had been a supporter of the arts throughout her life. The funeral on Wednesday at 3 p.m. Jack described as "dull," with few references to his mother in prayer, and the cryptic remark: "no 'ashes' at the grave."

After the funeral, the family was told to decide what they wanted from the house, marking the items with stickers for identification as all would be assessed. On Thursday Jane and Jack left for Kirkridge with china, crystal, pictures, sterling tableware, a guitar, viola, fiddle, and banjo, plus books and letters from his father. "Ring and brooch still lost," he wrote on the 27th, and, indeed, in the official list of what was in the house at his mother's death, the diamond ring is listed as missing, but there is no mention of a brooch.

On the 28th Jack was back at Kirkridge for a retreat on "Gain from Other World Faiths" led by M.M. Thomas from Union Theological. The group worked well on logs and stones for an under-porch patio for the Buciarski residence. He wrote that he was "bushed" after his mother's death and little sleep.

George Buciarski, a Polish immigrant, and his German-born wife Gisela had been one of the many couples Jack brought over as Displaced Persons after World War II. They had been temporary residents at Kirkridge before being set up in a house near Bangor, and now George returned to a one-year contract for maintenance work on the property. He, his wife, and two children moved into the Lower House, one of the newer houses on the property. George agreed to work under Horace Brewer three days a week and Ans van der Bent for the rest of the week while his wife would clean the Lodge during the week, all for $400 weekly.

Construction on the mountain was booming that fall. The farmhouse had four bedrooms added; the Hermitage was transformed from the Platts' chicken coop into a four-bedroom structure; a garage was constructed behind the Hermitage to house the truck and machinery; a new access road was added; fields were leveled; wells were deepened, and septic tanks were installed in Darwood, the Farmhouse, and the Upper House.

According to Board Minutes for October 23-4, Joe Beers was promised a trade for the "Ross Tract," 22 acres where 191 crossed the Ridge for four and a half acres to build a 60-foot strip for a roadway across Kirkridge's 41-acre ridge-top plot at the school site. These same Minutes note that the Board saw Jack's absence from Kirkridge as a "continuing handicap," and he promised "a radical clearance of summer calendar in 1967" and resignation from several of his non-Kirkridge responsibilities.

Plans for both the school, referred to as SAKI (the School at Kirkridge, Incorporated), and the alcoholic rehabilitation center, which would be known as Turning Point, were now in full swing. Mr. C. David Hudnut, head of the school task force, visited 38 schools in New England and the Middle Atlantic states, interviewing teachers and headmasters about how religion was interpreted at their campus, what approach was taken to curriculum, and how authority and discipline were perceived. It was crucial for the Board to decide whether SAKI would be "an early college, grades 11-14?" When a Board member suggested that, as to Christian approach, the school should "affirm and celebrate the Christian faith, without compulsion or anxiety," there was general agreement that this was an apt formula.

Thanksgiving 1966 found 18 people around the Farmhouse table, with Ans van der Bent asking the blessing. That weekend Jack wrote in his diary that he still had no church, that he was considering joining SANE (Committee for a Sane Nuclear Policy) for a national rally, and that he looked "tired and like grim death."

Instead of attending the rally, Jack decided to go to Pittsburgh the following day with Jane and Jim Loughery, one of the Kirkridge residents, for two days of "R & R." While in Pittsburgh, they loaded a 16-foot van with dishes, pictures, two pianos, and more books. Jack visited his Aunt Massa and wondered if a seminary couple would actually live in the family home. (They never did.)

On the 29th the three picked up another man at the Veterans' Hospital, and by 5 p.m. they all headed to Kirkridge over snowy roads, unloading items from the station wagon and truck into the garage until well after midnight. "Whew!" was Jack's one-word summary of the trip. According to Jack's diary entry for December 5, the two pianos never arrived at Kirkridge, and he discovered that two of his mother's vases had been sold by one of the drivers for $15. No mention of the pianos appears after this entry, but they did eventually turn up on the mountain.

As another Christmas approached, Jack bragged that his cards (all 480 of them) were sent out early, with a picture of the Celtic cross in the Lodge window.

28. John Oliver Nelson (JON) looking to
horizon through window of the Lodge.

The card read "Far horizons to you at Christmas!" and carried the
message of his mother's death and the proposed school's opening. He
used a "red edge to help cheer it up!" and noted that he used "lots of
double-line Esterbrook pens" to sign in his inimitable handwriting.
On Christmas Eve the snow began to fall, and with Jane ready to
serve a turkey dinner to Jack, Rick, and his friend Mike Turner (who

worked at Kirkridge), a carload of snowbound people with children landed on their doorstep.

Jack "lugged" the baby to the Farmhouse in the snow, and Jane fed them all the turkey dinner she had prepared for her own family. Stockings were hung on the hearth for the children, and with the snow continuing to fall, Rick, unable to get back to the base, called a buddy to cover for him so he would not be considered AWOL.

By Christmas Day the snow was 18 inches high, but the road was ploughed, and Jack asked the Farmhouse visitors to please make plans to leave. Ignoring his suggestion of imposition, they stayed until 4:00 the 26th, angry that they were being put out of a free lodging with phone, where they had hoped to stay for an extended period. Jack's final note on the "nervy" visitors: "They left a duck!"

The situation of squatter families or single drifters "dropping in" at Kirkridge was already a problem and would only get worse in the ensuing years. As Jack tallied up the Christmas gifts sent in from Kirkridge donors, he rejoiced that he could lower the demand note in New Haven to $27,000. New Year's Eve was spent with Jane and Rick's girlfriend at the Irwins' home, where they enjoyed a steak dinner. Jack's last entry for 1966 reads: "No bang. Whimper!"

The major decisions for January of the new year included deciding who would be the new headmaster of SAKI and when would the school be ready for students. At this point, William D. Scott, mayor of Bangor, was the number one choice as headmaster. Construction for Buchanan, the residence being built for students, was underway, and a road was being leveled as weather permitted. On January 6, 1967 Jack officiated at a wedding at Kirkridge between Mike Turner and Carmel Rae Sabatini. Pictures were taken, good food provided, and blackberry cordial served. It was a joyous occasion on a snowbound mountain and the harbinger of a new emphasis at Kirkridge: human relationships.

Nearly a year before, the Sycamore Community (the nation's oldest house church in State College, Pennsylvania) and Board Member

Rustum Roy (with his wife Della) presented a book to the Kirkridge Board tentatively entitled *Sex Ethics* (later renamed *Honest Sex*). Seeing the sexual revolution that caught fire across America in the 60s, these two author-scientists from Penn State University began to compile data on the sexual behavior of believers, culminating in this book, which they wanted Kirkridge to publish, with all proceeds going to Kirkridge.

With a few Board members nervous about some of the more conservative Kirkridgers' perception of this book, *Honest Sex* came out with a Kirkridge copyright, but with the caveat: "Kirkridge, Inc. does not necessarily approve all views expressed here, but offers this discussion as an important contribution to the current reevaluation of Christian sexual attitudes and principles." The authors, together with the Sycamore Community "to which they belong and which materially helped to prepare, write, and revise it," dedicated the book to "the sexually disadvantaged, perplexed, or arrogant in our time, for whom Christendom and the society begotten by it, has shown little concern and given small light." Kirkridge had always attempted to meet needs unmet by the institutional Church, and at this point in history, human sexuality was high on the list.

In May, Kirkridge planned a 25th anniversary celebration, and with the hiring of Keith Irwin as program director, a new ministry would become the hallmark of Kirkridge for the next decade. Keith and Jane arranged for Dr. O. Hobart Mowrer, noted group therapy leader, to come to Kirkridge for four days in October to participate in an Integrity Therapy Workshop.

Within a year Kirkridge would be the East Coast center of the Human Potential Movement–but in early 1967, with a war raging in Vietnam and with buildings being constructed all over the mountain, the Kirkridge Board realized that the most important person on the Board may have been Muriel Gross, a New York attorney, and legal counsel to Kirkridge for many years.

The first problem she brought to the attention of the Board in March was that Kirkridge was building a school on property it did not own—even though Jack was providing the money and land for the school. He promised to solve this problem by the next Board meeting, turning over the land to Kirkridge.

A second problem that Ms. Gross called to their attention was that state educational construction requirements had to be met when building a school. Again, the Board promised to comply with all state regulations. Finally, it was agreed to pay for legal counsel when needed regarding the formation of separate corporate entities all on the same property: Kirkridge itself, SAKI, and Turning Point.

By May the Board had rewritten the Charter for Kirkridge, reflecting its new emphases away from clergy education and more towards lay programs. The new wording read: "To engage in a non-profit religious, charitable and educational program for the purpose of relating Christian insight to secular life by means of experimentation, study and research and by providing direction, guidance, facilities, personnel, funds and other means to this end."

The constantly revolving personnel at Kirkridge continued to change: David Hudnut took a job teaching English at Germantown Friends High School; Hugh Latham, a friend of Jack's for many years, left the Smithsonian to come to the school, living at the almost-completed Buchanan House. David Johnson would leave his position teaching sociology at Bethel College in St. Paul, bringing his wife and two small children to join Hugh Latham in Buchanan House.

Gilbert Collyer, having been involved with Turning Point from the beginning, also joined the staff. And finally, Mrs. Aliki Turner and her son Charles would come in July from Istanbul, Turkey, she to be "'house mother' in care of various Kirkridge facilities." James Loughery, currently living in a trailer on the Kirkridge property with his wife, would join the maintenance staff, she performing secretarial tasks. With new people in place, Jack and Jane left on May 1 for Puerto Rico and a well-deserved two-week rest. Rick even managed to visit with them, bringing a friend with him from the base. While there, Jack called, asking that more stock be sold: 300 for Kirkridge, 100 for him "so we can live."

Upon their return, Jack and Jane continued in their efforts to build a community on the mountain; the group met for prayer each day at 1:30 p.m. and held meetings at which all were invited to provide input. Designed to promote "teamwork and fellow-feeling," the end result often led to disagreement about everything from programs to housecleaning methods, but Jack and Jane persevered.

In July the couple went again to Chautauqua, coming home in August to find one of Jack's former house guests at New Haven there, and visibly drunk. The men got into a serious fight, which Jack won, "sore" but relieved to have removed the man from the premises. Jack was able to get back to writing and preparing for his retreat entitled "Minister as Witness Among Witnesses" at the Naperville Evangelical Theological Seminary to be held August 30-31.

On Labor Day, Jack went once more to Mt. Saviour Monastery in Pine City, New York, for the annual Institute on Spirituality. There he shared the program with famed artist Sr. Corita Kent ("sparrow-like and intense"), Douglas Steere, Bernard Häring, Godfrey Dieckmann, OSB, Bernard Cooke, and Father Damasus of Mt. Saviour. Jack hurried home, "glad and fulfilled." "I'm no monk!" he wrote upon his return.

On September 23, 1967 Kirkridge held its first outdoor communal meal with games on the lawn. Hot dogs, rotisseries, and frisbees were the big hits of the day. As the month came to a close, huge stones were rolled into place for the Buchanan parking lot, but the hoped-for opening of the school for that fall did not become a reality. At the Board's request, Jack presented his long-range goals for Kirkridge at the October 1 meeting:

- To link Christian devotion and theology with action for social change,
- To extend and deepen disciplined small group retreat,

- To uphold clergymen and laymen in their contemporary roles,
- To enlarge the use of good art forms in Christian contexts,
- To set up pilot projects in Christian witness.

The Board approved all of Jack's goals, with the exception of his desire to build a "small place of worship" in 1968. Even though Jack argued that this modest building, as planned, would provide "a room for daily staff devotion, an unobtrusive artistic witness at Kirkridge which is otherwise frugal, and a spot to which retreatants or guests could withdraw for quiet devotion during and between retreats"–Jack never fulfilled his wish of building a chapel on the mountain.

With the Board meeting over, Jane and her sister Georgina Bone, visiting from Saskatoon, went into New York City, and had their bags stolen from the VW, which marred the trip. Rick finally came home from Vietnam on October 16, to his parents' delight. On the 22nd Jack and Rick discussed his future, Rick agreeing to begin the Walter Gapp Extension School in February. Other happy news that month for Jack was that he at last completed the second chapter of his manuscript for **Dare to Reconcile** and that James and Carlyn Loughery asked him and Jane to be godparents for their newborn daughter, Rebecca Ann.

By November the heat was on at Turning Point, but they were without water. And on November 9th, Jack wrote, "I out $125,000 for school?!"-- but that cost would only continue to rise. The next day Jack left for the Association Press Board meeting in New York, where he wrote he'd stay on until February, 1969, when a friend left the Board.

A Monroe City Ministerial Association gathering at Kirkridge on the 14th was successful, but Jack kept trying to get away to complete his overdue manuscript to little avail. "O day succeeds day *sans* work done!" he wrote the day before Thanksgiving. But with eight gathered around the Thanksgiving table, and a new group of Square

Pegs coming in after this, Jack got back to Chapter Five of **Dare to Reconcile**–the book due October 1. This particular Square Pegs retreat was noteworthy because, as Jack wrote, for the first time Roman Catholic seminarians would gather with their Protestant colleagues.

One of the Louisville seminarians present announced that he would leave the seminary to enlist in the army, a reminder that the war was far from over. For the next two weeks Jack worked on the manuscript, calling on the 18th to say it would be late. Christmas dinner was celebrated early on December 18 so that he could leave for a talk in Nashville on "Church=Memory and Expectation." Before he left, he called to sell 200 more Gulf shares to pay the bills.

In the last Ridgeleaf for 1967, Jack sent New Year's greetings from "those who live and work here": the van der Bents, Nelsons, Irwins, Gresses, Buciarskis (with new baby), Johnsons (with new baby), Hugh Latham and Richard Otto (new hire for Turning Point), intern Harry Wagner, the Lougherys (with new baby), and the Turners. With three infants and young Charles Turner on the mountain, new buildings springing up everywhere, and a new year before them, hope permeated the winter of 1968.

For Jack and Jane, that new year began with a trip to Spain, where Jack completed his Christmas cards, "until eyes gave out," spending $45 for postage to send from a foreign country.

Two memorable parts of the trip were the three Kings processing from the seaport to the cathedral, where they went for the service on January 6, and meeting a "wondrous" classical guitarist named Jose Cobos. With Jack's love of music, he encouraged Cobos to come to America to play, but soon the musician and his manager believed Jack would be their patron: a definite problem in translation.

Jane and Jack flew from Spain to Paris, where Jane discovered upon calling home that her father, John Bone, had died the previous day of a heart attack at age 83. The couple called the Irwins to send flowers, stayed on to visit a few monasteries and cathedrals, then flew to England, did the prescribed sightseeing, visited Jane's cousin, then they were off to JFK, with Jane flying from there to Saskatoon to be with her family. When Jack returned to Kirkridge on the 18th, he immediately ordered that more Gulf shares be sold.

The trip to Europe so soon after his mother's death and marred by the death of his father-in-law moved Jack to reflect on his own aging and his urgency to foster a deeper mystical life. Once again, he resolved to build a chapel on the mountain, but prior commitments left Jack little time for real reflection. Two days after returning from Europe, he was off to the airport for a flight to Los Angeles and then to Phoenix and another visit to the Verde Valley School.

The real reason for his trip west, a retreat at Colorado Women's College in Denver, gave Jack a chance to visit both Christ of the Desert retreat center and monastery of the Holy Cross in Abiquiu, New Mexico, where he gave his talk on "Eagerness." Jack spent a day at the Ghost Ranch Conference Center, sponsored by the Presbyterian Church USA, also in Abiquiu, and he visited the Benedictine Monastery at Albuquerque before heading to Denver. He returned to Kirkridge on the 29th, looking forward to meeting Jane, who was also just in from Canada.

The next day he was back in New York giving a lecture at the Jewish Theological Seminary, "Are There Hopeful New Experiments in Church Structure?" ("A few," he noted in his diary, but failed to list them.) Receiving 500 more shares of Gulf stock from his mother's inheritance the next day helped to pay immediate bills, but major debts continued to rise along with the new buildings. Jack had spent $176,000 on Kirkridge in 1967, and the end was not in sight.

In February Rick started at Diablo Valley Jr. College in California, raising Jack's hopes that after two years Rick could enroll for the third year in a "real college." Hopes for controlling spending–or traveling–seemed more remote. Before the March Board meeting, Jack had been to Lycoming College, the National City Church in Mt. Vernon, Virginia, Moravian College (which paid him $400 for the talk, to his delight), and finally his annual trip to Earlham College, where he was a valued speaker and teacher.

On February 22nd, he traveled to Philadelphia to evaluate Presbyterian seminarian exams in the Witherspoon Building. He got home late on the 24th after "slogging" through 56 papers, only to discover that his Aunt Massa had died. He and Jane left for Pittsburgh and another family funeral.

29. JON addressing the Scranton Council
of Churches, October 19, 1968

30. Scranton Council of Churches meeting October 19, 1968

America in the 1960s burned both with passion and promise, yet the young, energetic President John F. Kennedy who took office in January of 1961 could not have foreseen how the decade would play out. The civil rights movement, which began in the late 50s, blossomed, but the first of four assassinations occurred with the death of President John F. Kennedy in November of 1963.

In February of 1965, Malcolm X was shot, and in 1968, America lost both Dr. Martin Luther King on April 4 and Senator and Presidential candidate Robert F. Kennedy on June 5. The riots that occurred after Dr. King's death left America bruised and beaten. And after the second Kennedy assassination, anger erupted, energizing the "end-the-war" movement, dashing hope over much of America's youth that a new era of peace and harmony had descended upon America and the world.

Despite the chaos that seemed to have taken over the country, Kirkridge and Jack Nelson went on believing that peace would come and the war end, that young people could still be attracted by the Gospel vision of service, and that humankind could still pursue the high ideals that had inspired the first Kirkridgers.

Thus, while cities were burning all across America, Kirkridge opened Turning Point with ten guests, and opened the School at Kirkridge, described in a *Ridgeleaf* in November 1966 as "an exhilarating glimpse of the Incarnation, in all teenage study and all choice of a teaching team to make world and Spirit real."

Jack's dream of a school on the mountain, in which both young men and women grades 10 and 11 from various social classes could learn in new and creative ways, was realized in the late summer of 1969, with the plan to add 12th grade the following year. Hugh Moore, Jr., an Easton architect, drew up plans for a $350,000 multi-purpose building for the school. But the prayed-for donors did not materialize.

In the *Ridgeleaf* for 6 October 1969, Jack wrote "for the first time since 1942 Kirkridge is out of money, next-to-bankrupt, on real subsistence." Further on, he noted that "the Board found in August that ambitious Kirkridge spending (in two years $200,000 for Turning Point, $100,000 for SAKI, $65,000 for Mull, $180,000 for staff) has used up almost every dollar of the Nelsons' treasure and benevolence."

Consequently, all salaries stopped October 1st, except the van der Bents'. Mayor William D. Scott, Jr. of Bangor was appointed controller by the Board. George Buciarski and Aliki Turner got other jobs. The Nelsons stayed on without salary. So did the Irwins until April.

The Ridgeleaf continued: "Jane McT. Nelson is the Director of the retreat and study center program, drawing on her ministry at Five Oaks in Ontario. She drew on her wide experience leading and coordinating retreats and her role as a United Presbyterian minister.... Financially we are 'broke': spiritually and program-wise, we flourish!"

With true Nelson optimism, Jack concluded that perhaps there was meaning in having to be frugal, simpler, as in the early days of Kirkridge. "Are we part of the answer to Vietnam and the poverty put-down and the Christian credibility gap?" he asked. "Real witness is a gift." And the gift of witness burned brightest in the Shalom Retreats that would become a staple of the new decade.

Turning Points

1970-1979

In some ways the new decade brought refreshed hope that with a bare-bones staff, Jack and Jane could continue to keep Kirkridge alive and well. While the school (begun in the fall of 1969) had put Jack "in debt," it had also led him to be "greatly fulfilled." At that time there were 43 students and six graduates.

Additionally, according to the *Ridgeleaf* of 1 February 1970, Turning Point had two dozen guests who had completed a four-week course on alcohol addiction. The course was designed to "educat[e] men and women, along AA lines with Christian insight." At a cost of $548 per person, the program showed real promise of providing a source of much-needed revenue.

But it was the Shalom Retreats, held monthly and led by Jerry and Elisabeth Jud, which became the hallmark events of the early 70s. Beginning on Thursday evening and ending on Sunday afternoon, these intense encounter group experiences, part of the Human Potential Movement, probably changed more lives than Turning Point.

Along with other retreat experiences on responsible communal life styles and Christianity among World Religions, Kirkridge continued to provide in a Christian setting the opportunity to explore questions of human sexuality, racial and gender inequality, and peacemaking in a country still racked by the Vietnam War.

In April of that year, 43 gathered at Skerryvore (one of the Kirkridge buildings Jack named for Inner Hebrides islands) to experience "one of the most variegated and passionate colloquies ever." Rustum Roy, Penn State professor and Board member, Edward Bennett, the Penn State chaplain, and Robert H. Rimmer, author of **The Harrad Experiment**, met with delegates from communes across the country. They discussed "sexual openness, the logic of nudity, the liberation of women and men as well," all in a Christian context. With an estimated 3,000 communes of six or more adults in America, Kirkridge became the only site where such questions were discussed within a religious perspective.

In late June of 1970, Jack summarized the energy of a renewed Kirkridge in *Ridgeleaf,* asking: "What's happening to Christianity?" With doom-criers responding that local churches must be replaced, he reflects that people are alienated, hostile, and fearful as never before. The "nuclear family" is inadequate and must be superseded by communes and freer sex. Secularism is strong and "spiritual forces" have little future; clergy, especially the ablest, are opting out; missionaries have become an anachronism; and worship and devotion are flooded out by guitars and choruses, Zen and "sensitivity."

Given this pervasive negativity, Jack wrote that Kirkridge faced these challenges with both traditional and contemporary forms:

- Dynamism for congregations, to renew koinonia [communion by intimate participation], team effort, solidarity;
- Distinctively Christian "encounter groups" to reorient persons, vocations, relationships;
- Upholding of both communes and family life, with New Testament realism about sex;
- Linking youth revolt with Incarnational claims, even in sect-type expressions;
- Probing updated roles of ministers, priests, laity, women;

- Witness abroad and at home, by dialog with non-Christians in humility and helpfulness;
- Worship.

"Can this retreat-and-study center in wide outreach, tackle all these?" Jack asked. "Board and staff urgently intend to."

Jack's diary for spring of 1970 reflects his ambiguity about his ability to raise money for Kirkridge outside of direct appeals through *Ridgeleaf*. An application for a Clement Stone Foundation grant lay unfinished. He bought plane tickets in March for Omaha and Cincinnati, but admitted that he delayed making the necessary contacts there. By May he had to decide if he should trade 18 acres of Kirkridge for a 100-foot right of way to the Beers tract to provide land for an office.

Real estate and financial decisions were put aside, however, by the excitement of having parents of the SAKI students for a buffet and tour the weekend of May 22. The students presented their artwork, sang madrigals, did a skit on *Animal Farm*, and discussed plans for a June trip to New York for nine of the seniors.

If Kirkridge seemed an idyllic retreat from the chaos that marked the rest of the country, this proved not to be the case. The student rebellion and anti-war fervor that marked many American campuses found kindred spirits at SAKI. Stroudsburg, with its easy access to New York City and Philadelphia, became a place where drugs were easily accessible–and the SAKI students had little difficulty finding them.

A few students were sent home for repeatedly breaking rules or drug use, and by the end of June, Jack wrote that while many thought of him as 55, he felt 85. The next day he wrote letters to 45 SAKI parents, "all typed by me," still confident that the school could be kept open.

That summer brought some needed peace, even though money was tight. Jane and Jack went back to New Haven to their former home, still being rented. They spent their annual vacation at the

Nelson home on Chautauqua Lake, and Jack even found a Series E United States savings bond that when cashed for $1,707 paid a sewage bill and allowed money for travel. As was his wont, however, Jack gave most of it away to a man living on the property who was in dire financial straits–again.

When the Board met in late August, Chairman Rustum Roy asked that with the Juds' pending departure, the Board attempt to secure stable leadership to provide the "encounter-undergirded-with-witness emphasis which is unique to Kirkridge," and asked that Jack write a *Presbyterian Life* article about how Kirkridge was using Esalen-type events in a Christian context. It was agreed that by spring of 1971 a colloquy would be held on the subject of Alvin Toffler's *Future Shock*, which was published that year.

The Board's decision to close Turning Point by September broke Jack's heart, even though all were sure that "encounter groups" would be more profitable. The encounter groups were powerful, life-changing initiatives to explore and find one's true inner self in a safe, supportive, Christian setting. SAKI was allowed to stay open at least another year, and on September 13, 27 boys and 20 girls began the fall semester.

By November of 1970, the Shalom Retreats had become so popular and the numbers grown so large that Jack wrote, "Our handsome Turning Point campus shifts now from alcoholism to a mounting program of Kirkridge Shalom Retreats and Marriage Marathons." Ten-day summer leadership programs in encounter groups mainly for pastors rounded out the new orientation at Kirkridge. The influence of Jane Nelson can truly be seen in this new direction. While Keith and Marian Irwin led most of the Marriage Marathons, reaching out to gays and lesbians began while Jane was director of programming at Kirkridge.

In addition, it was Jane who originated the free weekends for the unemployed who could get to Kirkridge. The healing of many people who'd been wounded by society and their respective churches is one of the great legacies of Kirkridge that continues to this day. Jane's gentle ways and gift for counseling helped many return to their churches and communities with renewed hearts.

The new year began with a rough start. Jack received a call that Jack's last living aunt, Bess, 87, was hospitalized. And Jane had gone to visit her family in Saskatoon.

The war news was equally depressing. Jack's years of working with peace groups intensified during these years. A founding member of the Fellowship of Reconciliation, he was now also active in WANACH (War-Nation-Church Study Group), founded in 1967 by Mennonite Paul Peachey and based in Washington, D.C. The Vietnam War was tearing America apart during these years, and Kirkridge not only held weekend retreats led by the Berrigans and other peace activists, but occasionally offered haven to men en route to Canada as war resisters. Kirkridge became an Underground Railroad of sorts.

The winter months brought a new $13,000 loan from the bank, Jack putting up 611 Gulf shares and 83 other shares as collateral. Now taxes and salaries could be paid. On February 2 Jack completed the Beers right-of-way land exchange agreement ("Give me $100, Ed."). Yet Jack agonized over not having completed the Student Prayerbook he had promised the Board, writing on February 12 that $7,000 of the $13,000 loan was already gone. The next day the SAKI board met, encouraging Jack to either submit the foundation grant or "raise $70,000." By March 5 the combined Turning Point and SAKI Boards met with the Kirkridge Board and voted to close the school. Jack's diary tells of tears all around: "I a bit numb over it all," he wrote.

In April of 1971, Jack and Jane drove to Pittsburgh to celebrate Easter with Bess. The highly anticipated spring *Future Shock* retreat was "shockingly attended." On the 21st Jack wrote that the staff was "sometimes grumpy, unreliable." He decided not to attend the 200,000 March on D.C. for the 24th. Spirits were low all around, yet retreatants still found their way to Kirkridge, seeking peace in the midst of a war-torn nation.

In June of 1971 the second and last class graduated from the School at Kirkridge. Sixteen students received their diplomas from Jack in his blue academic robe, with graduates admitted to Yale, Vassar, Goddard, Oberlin, Antioch, Northwestern, Duquesne, Georgetown, Rocky Mountain, Ohio, Beloit, Kirkland, Penn State, Drake, and Windham. In an effort to provide a racial and cultural mix, scholarships had been given to some of the students, providing an "extraordinary mix," but also creating a colossal debt of $80,000 for scholarships that were never funded by foundation grants as hoped.

Transfers were arranged to other boarding schools for those who had not completed their senior year, and it was with a heavy heart that Jack's dream of a thriving school on the mountain ended, like so many other projects, in debt. The Board sent out a letter on July 31 to "1200 Kirkridgers," telling the faithful that with Turning Point and SAKI now closed, "we are back to the great thrust begun in 1942 for wholeness in Church and wholeness in persons," adding that the total debt is "about $160,000" with annual costs (and no salaries for the Nelsons) coming in at $96,000.

The mailing list was cut in half to save on costs. And a plea for Kirkridgers to help defray the debt promised that donations would help to carry on "our unique Christian contribution in the encounter-group movement, . . . authentic spirituality and distinctive new paths and patterns of Christian living."

Since Shalom Retreats and Marriage Marathons still had waiting lists, Kirkridge's next venture was Re-Evaluation Counseling, training leaders in combining "human-potential processes with New Testament perspectives." Mary McCabe, recently at Pendle Hill, brought this newest week-long training experience to the mountain. And added to these regular events, Kirkridge that year had Charles Davis, Brother Frank of Taizé, Ernest Campbell, and Pierre Roche leading more traditional weekend retreats.

In late summer of 1971 another of Jack's dreams came true. The Qahal Community moved into the Farmhouse in September. Qahal, Hebrew for "congregation of God's people," was comprised of several young families whose fathers had outside professional jobs and who shared common meals and informal daily worship. Peopled mainly by men and women who had been in Catholic religious communities, this new effort at a Christian commune on the mountain lightened the heart of John Oliver Nelson, as he now had a group that might reflect the Iona Community at last.

With the Vietnam War still raging, Kirkridge never forgot its peace mission, a direction that Kirkridge had embraced from its earliest days. Paul Mayer, instrumental in the Berrigan brothers' defense, led "bedroll youth" in August, discussing non-violence and peace-making. In the fall, James Forest of the Catholic Peace Fellowship "pointed a bedroll youth retreat to poverty (really poor, and poor in spirit) and new justice." That same fall Kirkridge hosted a "Science Becomes Theology" colloquy, bringing in both theologians and "top-flight scientists," such as Roger Shinn, Harold Schilling, Ian Barbour, Gerhard Barsch, and particularly Carl Friedric von Weizsacker, All were invited by the committee headed by Rustum Roy and Ernest Hawk of Penn State's Sycamore Community.

By mid-autumn, the two Qahal couples moved from the Farmhouse into Staffa and Eriskay (both named for Scottish islands), and the residents on the mountain increased by the month. Pierre Roche, sociology professor at nearby East Stroudsburg State College (ESSC) (and who also gave yoga retreats), lived at Lorne. John and Rose Bartlett were at Barra; Bob Godfrey, sculpture teacher at ESSC, and Boykin Reynolds, a former dorm counselor at SAKI, lived downstairs at Eriskay.

31. Jack and Walter Dend (of Corning) at Eriskay

32. "Tobermory" 1972 (now Turning Point's sleeping quarters)

A former SAKI student, Vernon Brown, lived in one of the trailers and became a cook for the retreatants, and Bob Weidner, who "sells and plays guitars," lived in the Folly. A Quaker Biblical theologian, Janet Shepherd from Pendle Hill, moved into the upstairs of the Farmhouse and became its hostess. Ruth and Andries van der Bent continued to make the traditional ceramic Celtic crosses. The now-abandoned powder storehouses in the woods became for hikers the unofficial hostel that never got built on the mountain.

Eventually one of the storehouses became the refitted home of the Kirkridge cook, her husband, and two small children. An added blessing that season was Rick's unexpected visit home over Christmas. Jack rejoiced at what might finally become his American Iona.

The 30-year anniversary of Kirkridge in 1972 did little to alleviate the financial crunch that never quite went away after Jack's inheritance dwindled, plus the winter brought two ice accidents that totaled both the blue and brown vans. When the thermostats failed in the Farmhouse, the cost was $2,800 in uninsured damage to replace the radiators after a sub-zero freeze. Miraculously, the spirit of Kirkridge was never dampened by the lack of funds. Programs continued and evolved. For instance, theologian and composer Sebastian Temple combined yoga with guitar-ballad singing. Marriage Marathons with the Irwins continued, as did Shalom Retreats with the Juds. The Irwins led Clergy-And-Wives Re-Enforcement Labs. Cora Logan offered a seminar-workshop on Kinestherapy, demonstrating new help for birth-defect and post-stroke patients. And, of course, Sir George MacLeod, "our patron," came from Scotland to celebrate the 30th anniversary on May 12. In the June issue of *Ridgeleaf,* Jack reflected on the sixty Kirkridgers called "to the hearth fires where our mountain witness began."

On June 10 Kirkridge hosted a SAKI reunion; 70 alumni/ae showed up, and six even stayed the night. A work-group of 33 from Mt. Penn painted and de-trashed the property for two donated days, and hope sprang anew that Kirkridge, with its "Next Thirty Years Fund," could thrive for three more decades. Jack wrote of his disappointment that his aunt was not interested at all in setting up an annuity for Kirkridge, but he and Jane were grateful for the $25 checks she sent for each of them.

With Rick returning home that summer, the whole family went to Chautauqua, including Jane's sister Margaret. They attended an opera and Mozart concert. "Chautauqua an idyll," Jack wrote, as it had been from the time of his childhood. In September Jack drove to Pittsburgh and visited his Aunt Bess. He also solicited four foundations for Kirkridge funds and even considered selling off part of the property to raise money.

On September 13 tragedy came to the mountain. Jack's dear friend and SAKI Board member, Bill Scott, 55, was killed at 6:00 p.m. in an automobile accident at Route 191. He and Jane went immediately to console his widow Edith. "I frivolous till Bill!" Jack wrote that night in his diary. The death haunted him for a long time.

In October Jack flew to South Bend for a talk at the Elkhart Biblical Seminary and rejoiced that the response to his 2,500 Chautauqua "Christmas cards" was reaping checks to help with the debt. Donated fruit and pussy willow trees from a local nursery brightened the property. Both Jack and often Jane were asked to preach at local churches in the area, as they had done since arriving at Kirkridge in 1962. In mid-August Jack, for example, had three separate services, 8:45, 10:10, and 11:15, all in the area but at different churches. That same month he was notified that he would receive the Sertoma International Exceptional Service to Mankind Award the following year.

In a letter to her mother, Jane wrote that Jack always made light of these awards, comparing them to a bathing beauty competition. In another letter to her family that month, Jane told of feeling safer on the mountain now that a former priest had asked to live there, acting as a security guard for the property. She recalled how in the previous year someone had shattered the glass upper door to the office and stolen all of the typewriters. Many items were taken through the years by the young men who turned up asking Jack for a place to stay or by drifters, who wandered through the Appalachian Trail and found unlocked doors.

The couple had Thanksgiving with Bess in Sewickley, as usual. While in Pittsburgh, Jack met with a lawyer trying to work out the tax difficulties he confronted in trying to sell part of the property. The following week Jack again bemoaned his health: "Front upper tooth does work its way out...arthritis three months in upper arm, partial plate has broken hook, moves around...."

The Board met the first weekend of December, and Jack raced from Kirkridge to North Bennington for the ordination of his niece Sheila's husband, Leo Hourihan. His brother Doug preached, and Jack gave the Call to Prayer. He returned to Kirkridge for the Board meeting, noting in his diary that the Board walked in snow to Blair House. The Christmas season brought days of rain, but on January 4, friends from Pittsburgh sent Kirkridge $5,000. Other Board members offered cash to help defray ongoing debt.

On January 13, 1973, Jack got the last of the 380 Christmas cards sent. The programs at Kirkridge continued to fill the buildings if not the coffers, and things seemed to be turning the corner with new donations. However, he was certainly not prepared for the next event.

On March 20, Jack had an automobile accident that left him with a splintered kneecap and sprained ankle that would cause him problems for the rest of his life. "I nearly killed myself," he wrote in his diary. This accident was caused by total brake failure, discovered when he tried to move a car left by one of the squatters (now in jail). However, it did provide a wake-up call for his habit of speeding: an activity played out both on and off the road.

Two days later, Jack was awarded the Man of the Year Award by the Sertoma Club at a banquet and testimonial dinner. His brother

Doug and sister-in-law, Maxine, joined members of the Board and local community for the award, yet Jack's stitched head, damaged leg and crutches made it a difficult evening. In a letter to her family, Jane recounted how Cliff Jones, Board Chair, talked about Jack's spiritual qualities and his genius for sharing them with others. "It was a great evening," she wrote, "and also it was great when it was over–given Jack's condition!"

33. Jane Nelson, Douglas and Dorothy Steere in 1973

In April of 1973, Jane went back to Saskatoon to visit her family and ailing mother, and JON went to the Trappist Monastery in Gethsemane, Kentucky, one of his favorite places of quiet and prayer.

On May 13 Jack officiated at the marriage of one of the former SAKI students (still a cook at Kirkridge), Vernon Brown, and Mary Rita Lenox at the Lodge. Jack had a difficult time getting the squatters to leave. They now inhabited the mountain and become a source of regular friction for Jane and Jack.

Rather than sending many of these "freeloaders" on their way, Jack, the eternally hopeful Good Samaritan, often paid rent at local residences for them until they could get their lives in order. Few did. But Jack, taking the Gospel seriously, believed that if people needed shelter, food, or employment, he was duty-bound to try to help them—even with money that by rights should have provided for his wife and himself—and for keeping Kirkridge out of debt.

Now that the inheritance and the "easy money" of the cashed-in stocks were almost gone, it became difficult for Jack to realize that the future of Kirkridge depended upon fiscal responsibility. For him, the simple mandate of helping a fellow in need when asked always seemed to supersede. As one former worker at Kirkridge remarked in an interview, "For Jack, there were no undeserving poor."

Jane extended her visit with her family into late May, and Jack, at the demand of the Board, tried to get some of the Kirkridge squatters to find other homes. When Jane came back with her sister Georgina that summer, one of the squatters became violent and slapped the son of a Kirkridge worker. Jane, frightened, left again for a few days, "distraught." It was a time of great tension on the mountain, but the tension extended to the country as well.

Gas was being rationed and the nation was mesmerized by the Watergate hearings, which Jack watched regularly when he was not traveling. Jane's friend, Sally Bailey, also came to live at Colonsay at this time, and this provided companionship and support for Jane when Jack was away, which was often.

Jack and Jane had now been co-directors of Kirkridge for ten years, and with the school and Turning Point's alcohol rehabilitation center closed, Jack, now 65, asked that the Board begin the search for a new director. In his earlier years, Jack believed that one should change jobs every five years, but he had been at Yale for fourteen years before coming to Kirkridge and now a decade as director of Kirkridge. The new transition to living at Kirkridge without being its director would hold new challenges for both Jack and Jane–and whoever was chosen to lead the retreat center.

The big news in Jack's diary for January 1974 was the gas shortage. With transportation to Kirkridge crucial to the success of its programs, the threatened rationing of gasoline would hurt their numbers for retreats and sponsored gatherings. In addition, living on a mountain made traveling to Stroudsburg for shopping or bus transportation necessary.

Jack had an assortment of used cars, some of which were being used by the staff, some by Jack and Jane, and some by the men who lived on the mountain and helped with odd jobs. His diary tells of almost humorous stories of running out of gas and having another person come with siphoned gas to fill the tank, thus disabling that car for a day or two. In short, the gas crisis didn't help the attendance at events, nor did it make Jack and Jane's travel plans any easier.

But Jack's travel plans were not completely stymied. He still gave retreats on the mountain and at various other sites, as did Jane. In early March he flew to Five Oaks, Ontario, where he had met Jane in 1954, to give a retreat for 27 with the theme, "The Whole Armor of God." On March 7 he and the committee interviewed candidates in Pittsburgh, and his diary entry for that day is poignant: "Am the jester at all these dull affairs? I do speak truth to power –and I don't wanna be the power, really. All are younger, and I did my job awhile ago."

Jack returned to Kirkridge with the renewed purpose of getting the squatters from the property, a task at which he was never quite successful. What was successful, however, was finding a candidate upon which the committee agreed on March 16. Robert Raines, author and United Church of Christ ordained minister, had been one of Jack's first "square pegs," and had applied for the position when he knew it was opened. Ernie Hawk, chair of the committee, asked if Jack and the committee wanted to interview other candidates, but Jack replied, "No, I say now. I'm sold."

Working out the terms of the transition took more than a day, however. The Board had applied to the Lilly Foundation to help with the salary requirements of a new director. Essentially, Jack and Jane had worked without pay, at least in the last few years. The original offer was $20,000 and a house, but Raines wanted $30,000 plus $6,000 for the house. "Is this a change of Kirkridge style?" Jack wrote, "Will Lilly buy this?"

In May Jack received his first TIAA pension check for $276.52. It seemed like a great deal to him. On June 10 Rustum Roy set up a conference call with Jack, Bob, and himself that lasted an hour, and two hours later the three went to the Lilly Foundation, which agreed on a $100,000 grant in two years. Bob had hoped for $163,000 in three years, but they were grateful for the grant. "Ah me, 'tis done," Jack wrote in his diary that night. The new director would begin on September 1, 1974.

On June 17 a local farmer donated ten sheep to Kirkridge, soon to get a new shepherd. Sheep had been on the mountainside from the beginning, providing both grass cutting and food for retreatants. Jack rejoiced that his sister Peg sent her usual $200 for the annual Chautauqua vacation. "Good gal," he wrote, and Jack, Jane, and two young men who had been staying with them, Tsuneo and Stan, drove to the place that next to Kirkridge Jack loved best, 10 North Avenue.

In August Rustum Roy led a retreat for 28 on Lifestyles for the Second Half, a theme that would become the hallmark of the Raines era at Kirkridge. Robert Raines came to the job with a true interest in mid-life transitions, and this fit in well with the years of emphasis on the Human Potential Movement. At mid-month, the FOR held its retreat at Kirkridge, an organization that remained close to Jack's heart all his life. William Stringfellow, frail and using a cane, gave the last retreat before Robert Raines became director.

In mid-September, 32 people in all came for the Board meeting at Turning Point. Bob and Cindy Hirni, who would be married on September 23, were introduced to the Board. Jack sat in on Friday evening, but missed the Saturday morning meeting. Even then he wondered if he would "find how to retire!" Jack's life after being the director was not essentially different from his life as director. Jane held the position of associate director under Bob, and Jack still helped with mailings, wrote for the *Ridgeleaf*, and occasionally led retreats.

One of Jack's passions throughout his life was the prison ministry. Just as he had always tried to help alcoholics (AA meetings still were held each Sunday evening at Kirkridge), Jack both visited prisoners and gave them money to "start over." Often an expensive and seemingly futile mission, Jack nevertheless practiced this work of mercy to the end of his life.

In November of 1974, for example, Jack made the front page of the **Bangor Daily News**, but not for a speech or award. A group of young men got into a fight, and at 3:00 a.m. he got the call asking if he'd put up $13,000 bail. The headline next day read: "John Oliver Nelson puts up $13,000 bail after rumble." It wasn't the sort of publicity that Kirkridge or the new director needed, but Jack never second thought his benevolence.

Another example occurred in 1978. For Christmas he sent money orders of $10 each to ten young men whom he had been trying to help but who ended up in prison for burglary, drugs, and/or assault. "I was in prison, and you visited me" (Mt. 25:36) was a Scriptural verse that Jack made a maxim for his life.

As 1974 drew to a close, Jack still was concerned about the property and future of Kirkridge. Though he could no longer make huge donations to keep it going, he hung new draperies and painted walls, aided by some of the young men he tried to help. On December

5 he drove to St. Joseph Cistercian Abbey in Spencer, Massachusetts, where a meeting hosted by Father Basil Pennington was held. He always enjoyed participating in the silence and prayer life of the Cistercian abbeys he visited, and this one was no exception. A new abbot was consecrated while he was there, and with Jack's life-long attraction to solemn liturgical events, he commented in his diary, "great sincere service–incense."

The new year brought a month-long trip to Europe for Jack and Jane, encouraged by the Board to finally leave the worries about Kirkridge's future behind. Beginning in Geneva with an ecumenical religious conference, they traveled to Paris, visiting cathedrals and the Louvre. They then traveled on to London, which Jack found "rushing and dull." Sightseeing throughout much of England, the pair next drove to Scotland and Iona, visiting friends along the way and buying tweed wool coats and jackets.

They spent six days with Jane's relatives, the family of Jack Bone, and then headed to Belfast, where they ran into "horizontal snow." Arriving in Northern Ireland with all the stores closed, they were hungry for the first time on the trip: "raisins and my crisps all eaten," Jack wrote. With tales of another IRA cease-fire after so much bloody death, Jack commented the situation was "all great tragedy of cowardice and violence." The couple went to the opera, the ballet, and "churches everywhere." On January 31, 1975 they arrived home, with Jack writing, "We'll bore everyone with our story."

By February 6 Jack had finished his report about the trip, and at lunch with Bob, he learned that a festschrift was being planned to honor him. Friends and colleagues from all over the world were asked to contribute essays not merely about Jack and his life work, but also that would have the "bifocal perspective that Kirkridge itself has–facing always towards both the world and the Church."

Titled *You're Alright Jack,* the journal asked authors to "set down in a few pages their best judgment on where the Spirit of Creative Ferment, the Cry, God, was breaking out in the world." John

A.T. Robinson, N. Gordon Cosby, Joseph F. Fletcher, Roger Shutz, John L. Casteel, and others wrote the first articles under the heading "Behold I am doing a new thing!"

The second part of the book, under the heading "Retrospect and Prospect for Kirkridge," was more specifically about Jack Nelson or the institution of Kirkridge, and had essays by Joseph E. and Edith Platt, Gerald J. Jud, Douglas V. Steere, and Robert Raines. Edited by Rustum Roy and Kathleen S. Mourant, the book came out after the May 3 celebration honoring Jack for his leadership and enormous financial contribution to Kirkridge for over three decades.

The early months of 1975 brought renewed worry about money and family problems. Wenley's wife Wera was undergoing cobalt treatment for cancer, and in April Jack's uncle, Paul Dodds, died of bone cancer. Given his dire financial situation, Jack considered cashing in all his remaining Gulf stock, but he thought better of it, cashing in only a part. Tiree, their residence, seemed always to be in need of some repair: a new roof, new steps, or a new paint job.

Jack talked to Board Chair Cliff Jones about what to do, wondering if he should sell Lorne and Tiree. Meanwhile, Kirkridge was also attempting to sell part of the land to help with the debt. But Jack's life went on as usual. He taught a last class of the semester at Drew University and gave up an FOR meeting to grade exams of Presbyterian seminarians. Around this time he also began a one-day-a-week fast for peace through the International FOR, the money saved being sent to Brussels for world hunger.

Jack walked the Ridge with Jane to celebrate her 58th birthday on April 20, and Ans van der Bent provided a cake. On May 3, Jack wrote, "Ach, MY DAY!" Surrounded by 20 "witnesses," mainly men and a few women who had been with Jack from 1947, and numerous friends, Jack reveled in the camaraderie, Bob Raines' prayer, the luncheon, and the "costly, grand" gift portrait given by his friends. The afternoon was capped by Bruce Gelser's planting flowers around Tiree. The joy of the day put financial worries aside for a time.

In June of 1975, JON returned to Princeton for his 45th reunion; then in July he and Jane took Tsuneo and Evan Cramb to Chautauqua after signing up Tsuneo for five fall classes at Northhampton County Area Community College. Jack twice addressed the DAR on "Women as Internationalists" at Chautauqua, but after Jane left with Evan, he and Tsuneo spent much of the time cleaning, washing windows, cutting trees and stacking wood. They left the house "ship shape," returning to Tiree, where Jack spent the day in the cellar widening the stairs.

By summer's end, Jane was downhearted at her associate director position at Kirkridge, but Jack told her to "hang in there!" They both went to Saskatoon in mid-August, but Jack left for Fergus Falls, Minnesota, the day after they arrived, getting stopped for another speeding ticket on the way and fined $37. Leaving for a visit with Bess in Pittsburgh, Jack wrote that he never went above the speed limit. The next day he returned to Kirkridge and a stack of "unpayable bills."

On September 10, Jane and Jack drove to Rochester, New York, for the dedication of the Howard Hanson Plaza. It was the first chance he had had to talk with his sister Peg, Howard's wife, in four years. The next day Jack went to Hazleton for a talk, followed by a retreat at Kirkridge for the New Brunswick Seminary titled "Your God Is Too Small." Feeling energized by this experience, Jack wrote about how the seminarians had discussed new dimensions of service versus prayer. He also led songs, a task that Jack loved immensely.

When the Board met that September, Cliff Jones asked the members to help with the finances, and Jack wrote that Jane was "unhappy with *all*." But what happened at that meeting would become another important chapter in the story of both Jack Nelson and Kirkridge. "I suggest Kirkridge Company idea," Jack wrote, and on November 9, he met with Rustum and Della Roy, Berit Lakey, Cliff Jones, and George Yoder to flesh out what this new Kirkridge "geographically dispersed community" might become.

Yet for Jack Nelson, the Company, while hopeful, hardly took up all his energy or thoughts. Worries about his Aunt Bess mounted. A phone call on October 2 revealed that she had found no companion, and her professed loneliness broke Jack's heart. In an effort to help with debts, Lorne was sold in October, 1975. Purchase of a new furnace for their home and taxes took almost all the money from the sale of Barra, however, and Jack remarked in his diary: "Too much given away."

But what was probably more painful than the money given away was the directorship of Kirkridge. Kirkridge was no longer in his control, and when he complained in his diary about potholes, deferred maintenance, or not liking the new colors of paint, one senses an underlying frustration that what had been his sacred mountain was now only a mailing address over which he had little say.

34. "Mull" November 1975 (now the
Nelson Lodge sleeping quarters)

The year ended with a quiet Christmas holiday, Jane and Tsuneo skating on the ice. Jack's Christmas card that year read: "Mary's world encircle you in joy, clear-eyed for '76." Yet he couldn't resist complaining in his diary that postage had now gone up to 13 cents at midnight. On the 27th, Jack fell on the ice, dislocating his shoulder, an injury that would trigger bursitis, causing him pain for months to come.

Jack's new year began with constant pain from his shoulder injury, and by mid-January Jane, discontent with her job, was in bed with a cough. On January 16, Jack decided to sell Gulf shares for $17,500. This still did not even cover the bills that continued to come in. On the 27th, Jane's mother, Mary Campbell Bone, died in her sleep at age 88. Jane traveled alone on Air Canada from JFK to be with her family. She stayed until the 9th of February, and, true to form, Jack almost forgot their anniversary on the 11th. "Forgot I'm wed," he wrote, but the two went to dinner at the Holiday Inn to celebrate.

In 1976 the Nelsons faced many pressing concerns: the new leadership at Kirkridge, health problems, and the constant worry about money. Yet Jack never lost his spirit. He kept the promise he made to the International FOR to keep a weekly day of fast and sent the $6 saved on food to Brussels for world hunger when he could afford it, Jack writing that it cleared his mind and simplified his schedule.

The new year brought both change and two important new movements to Kirkridge. Jerry and Elisabeth Jud had their last Shalom for Clergy and Spouses in January, ending a fruitful seven-year affiliation with Kirkridge to open their own Shalom Mountain Center in the Catskills. Three couples would carry on the Kirkridge Shalom experience: Jim and Jane Miller, John and Dede Levering, and Dennis and Susan Harrison.

That February, Malcolm Boyd and Keith Miller drew 105 weekend retreatants to the mountain to discuss human sexuality, a topic that had been integral to Kirkridge since the 1960s. With the theme, "Where Is Your Struggle?" men and women discussed their difficulties with Christianity and sexuality, especially the alienation that gays often felt within Christian churches.

Kirkridge became, and still remains, a welcoming place of acceptance for gay and lesbian Christians of every denomination. For Jack, spreading this message became his new passion. When he attended conferences, he would often note in his diary that he spoke on this topic in lectures or privately to small groups. Kirkridge and certainly Jack Nelson wanted gays and lesbians to know that they could come to Kirkridge without judgment.

A second innovation was the formation of the Company at Kirkridge. The Company at Kirkridge, which began with inspiration at a Board meeting in the fall of 1975, was designed to give new life to Jack's original vision for Kirkridge in the early 1940s.

With a new director at Kirkridge and an increased demand for fiscal responsibility, what began as a movement for power in the Church gradually transformed into a retreat center that would attract a new group of people. The cost of programs necessarily increased, and the programs offered now often reflected mid-life issues, the main interest of the new director. This new direction, while ultimately saving Kirkridge as a viable center, came at a high cost. With Jack's role greatly diminished, many of the original Kirkridgers no longer felt the close connection they had previously. Many continued to support this revered spot that had been so influential in their spiritual lives.

The Company, Jack hoped, would keep his original dream alive. At the January Board meeting, the decision to launch this new effort was affirmed, and Berit Lakey and the planning committee of Cliff Jones, Ernie Hawk, Rustum Roy, George Yoder, Jack and Jane Nelson, and the Rainses designed what they hoped would be a permanent nucleus of persons committed to the inward-outward journey and the challenge of Picket and Pray. In March 1976 the *Ridgeleaf*'s lead essay aptly described the Committee's hopes:

The Company at Kirkridge is getting ready to be born. The idea of a congregation of people committed to the Kirkridge quest for inner light and outward action has been stirring our imaginations for a long time. At its meeting in January the Board decided that it is time to test the viability of such a "congregation" that would gather at Kirkridge several times a year.

The Company at Kirkridge will be a worshipping community bringing together both those who need more outside support and stimulation for their work in local congregations, and those who are not participating actively in a church at present. Members will come from a variety of church backgrounds and from a wide geographical area.

We hope it will become a community of men and women who can freely share their struggles and their insights, and where souls, psyches, minds and bodies can be challenged and nurtured. For many of us Kirkridge has been such a place of growth and integration. The Company will provide a context for continuity and commitment.

Tentative plans include a number of weekends of worship and fellowship where real Meeting can take place, as well as 'Cathedral Events" of a more formal nature when special leadership is brought in to share insight with us. It is quite possible that as the Company takes shape, a common discipline will be developed by members.

With a cost of only $15 for the weekend, the committee limited enrollment because of space concerns. That April brought more than 70 "pilgrims" from seven states to Turning Point, with "singing, sharing, planning, praying, praising, and protesting," according to the May *Ridgeleaf.* The newly christened Company "began to forge a covenant for life together—and apart!" Deciding to hold the first Cathedral Event in late August, the planning committee linked Bishop John A.T. Robinson's week-long Institute on the New Testament with the Company's weekend. The Kirkridge Company would never become a "permanent nucleus," but it would last more than two decades, outliving both Jack and Jane.

What often seemed like frenetic travel and activity for Jack actually provided Kirkridge with possible speakers and retreat leaders. In the spring he traveled to Bucknell University in Lewisburg for that purpose, and a Holy Week retreat at Mt. Saviour Monastery in Elmira, New York, became an occasion to try to get an AA facility founded there with its farm possibility–but that plan proved unsuccessful.

In late April, Jack was disappointed that only one square peg, Drew's Diana Vale, turned up for the seminarians' retreat. Early summer brought Jack and Jane together for a retreat at Kirkridge on Scripture and a workshop on dreams. Ultrasound treatments proved unsuccessful on Jack's shoulder, but eventually he found medication to help with the pain. Wenley and Wera came back from their trip to Europe in May, and after a SAKI reunion in June, Jane announced on June 27 that she would be stepping down from her position on September 1.

35. SAKI reunion on June 19, 1976 (Jack on right, first row)

As usual, Jack went to Chautauqua on July 20 with Jim Loughery, who shared the driving, but when Jim returned on a bus after a few days, Jack mused, "Can I be alone any more? Need hangers-on or Jane?" Chautauqua, however, provided both cultural and spiritual resources, and Jack eagerly awaited Jane's arrival, delighted that he could at last do six pushups. Nothing could dampen the spirit of summer at Chautauqua. Once again finding the house on the lake dirty, with one of the windows broken, Jack hired five women to clean before Jane arrived.

In late August 1976, Bishop John A.T. Robinson led a Scripture Institute for 80 participants, and, as planned, the weekend following the institute was the inaugural cathedral event for the Company at Kirkridge. Jack delighted in the number of attendees, of whom "32 or so were RC."

With great joy, the new Company prayed, sang, and discussed what direction the group might take. Eleanor Walker of Grail, Bishop Robinson, Jack and Jane, and more than a few Board members celebrated the final liturgy with the "wondrous" flute and recorder music of Philip Dietterich. With a Steering Committee of eleven selected, a newsletter planned, and the tea and symphony tradition upheld at Tiree, Jack wrote in his diary that night, "A good crew. So do we have a 'Company'?" Yes, the Company planned to meet four times a year at Kirkridge, and Jack and Jane were glad for this new venture in keeping the vision alive.

September on the mountain was always a glorious time because of the natural beauty of the surrounding woodlands, but the month ended sadly when Wenley called to tell them that Wera, 63, had succumbed to the cancer she had been fighting for the past few years. Jack commented that her September 30 service was poor, and she deserved better, as she was "great in many ways."

In October Jack and Jane drove to New Haven to celebrate the 275th anniversary of Yale University and stopped to visit Doug and his wife Maxine, called "Jerry" by the family. Twenty-four Campus

Chaplains met at the Farmhouse on October 11, with Jack preaching on the theme of eco-justice. With great joy Jack and Jane welcomed Rick and his girlfriend after not seeing him for more than a year. The young couple visited Bess in Pittsburgh and then drove back to Kirkridge to say good-bye.

The annual retreat for seminarians at Colonsay in November brought more happiness to Jack because he felt this work was at the heart of the original mission of Kirkridge. Thanksgiving 1976 found only three guests around the Nelson table, but the excitement of preparing for Jane's imminent trip to Ireland made for happy conversation.

The day after Thanksgiving Jack officiated at the marriage of Jean Slates Hawk and long-time friend and former Board member, Ernie Hawk, shortly before another Company at Kirkridge weekend gathering. Twenty-eight companions discussed Incarnational Theology and its transformative power, while enjoying the traditional tea and symphony quiet Saturday afternoon at Tiree. All signed Jane's banner that she would be taking to Northern Ireland the next day.

36. "Tea and Symphony" at Jack and Jane
Nelson's Tiree dining room in Tiree.

Before the last Company member left the mountain, Jack was rushing Jane to Kennedy Airport for the Journey of Reconciliation. Dubbed the Northern Ireland Peace Movement, this effort was triggered by the deaths of three young children of Anne Maguire on the streets of Belfast when a car, with the driver shot and killed, careened into the family. Anne's sister Mairead and Betty Miller inspired a movement with the words, "Enough's enough." Women particularly, from all over the world, came to join these two brave women who walked the streets of Northern Ireland praying for peace between the Catholics and Protestants. They were awarded the Nobel Prize for Peace that year for their efforts. Jane, her health improved, was impassioned to join them, and upon her return on December 6, Jack noted the number of times she had been quoted in news reports of the marches (40). The experience lifted both their spirits after a difficult year.

The new year came in with a wintry blast across the eastern half of the country. Jack visited his aunt on New Year's and then drove with Jane from Pittsburgh to Richmond, Indiana, and the Quaker Earlham School of Religion, where he served on the Board and often led workshops and classes. Now that he and Jane were free of the directorship of Kirkridge, they could travel together and even stay for extended periods of time. This first month of 1977 Jack led a class of 12 Clear Creek Friends (and eight audits) in "recollection, liturgy, and power." He completed his treasured Christmas cards and notes between sessions.

JON and Jane drove in deep snow to New Harmony, Indiana, to a Friends meeting on Sunday morning, and by Friday the snow had risen to over a foot with the temperature dropping daily to below zero. Jack worked all week with Clyde Johnson, who was beginning a Quaker intentional community, inspired by Iona and Kirkridge. According to his web site, in 1966 Johnson heard Jack give a speech in which he expressed the need "for places of concern, acceptance, relaxation, worship and quiet study in our hectic and harried world," and Ichthys

House was born. Jack's classes of Quakers were interspersed with meetings of the Yokefellow Institute Board, while Jane participated with worship services and group discussions.

From Richmond the couple traveled to South Bend and a few days with the First Methodist Church group. Jane "fine," spoke of her Ireland trip, but with the temperature dropping to 18 below, Jack and Jane drove back to Richmond for the completion of the class, which all passed, and then on to Indianapolis for the Carmelite Institute on Spirituality that he tried to attend annually.

By Monday, February 7, 1977 JON and Jane found themselves back visiting Bess and then on to Kirkridge, arriving in "high snows." Jack, "listless and sick" for the next six days, was glad to be back in his own bed. Trying to answer stacks of mail and getting back into the day-to-day tasks at Tiree (Jack and Jane's home in Kirkridge), Jack once again forgot his February 11 anniversary, but he made it up by giving Jane the rather un-romantic but appreciated gift of $200 house cash.

On Thursday of that week, they celebrated the 20th anniversary of the van der Bent's arrival at Kirkridge with a small dinner party. Unfortunately, the deep freeze surrounding the mountain retreat made Jack think that perhaps he was coming down with the flu. By Friday, he was feeling well enough to drive to Maryland's Dayspring Retreat Center, where sunshine and green grass served as a tonic. He spoke to the Foundry United Methodist Church group on Biblical memory, and Jane led the worship service and communion. They were back home by 11 that Sunday evening.

Spring brought more talk of land sales and disputes over taxes on land already sold. Bill Cohea encouraged Jack to build a chapel so there would be worship at Kirkridge, a dream Jack had from the beginning. Yet this concept of Church as building, while seductive, failed to grasp Jack's theology of the Church as the people of God.

One of the fondest memories many early Kirkridgers recall was the retreat liturgy around the dining room table, using ordinary utensils for daily meals as liturgical vessels. This Incarnational Theology, so dear to Jack's heart, never completely erased his dream of a chapel where daily worship could be held. While the rebuilt cathedral on Iona was the heart of the island, plans for a chapel once again evaporated for Kirkridge.

In April Jack made the decision to sell to the Department of Environmental Resources a right of way through the property, which sits on the Appalachian Trail, providing not only much-needed cash but the promise that the land could not be sold to developers for hotels or casinos, a fear that Jack had held since purchasing Kirkridge.

By mid-month Jane began a special Homala diet (no sugar, coffee, or tea), and for her 60th birthday, which Jack remembered, she received a watch, an afghan, and a special dinner at the Fernwood Hotel. On the 23rd she flew to Saskatoon to spend a month with her family. Jack led a retreat for retreat directors and continued the struggle over the taxes for the ten acres sold in 1976. As tax season approached once again, Jack wrote in his diary that it was lucky Jane was away. Despite financial problems for Kirkridge, renovation of the Lodge and Colonsay provided more and better accommodations for guests.

From May 5 to 9 in 1977, Kirkridge held its first retreat specifically for gay and lesbian Christians. Jack noted in his diary that 90 had signed up, 12 of them women and two African Americans. Roman Catholic and Protestant clergy and laity came. Led by then Jesuit Father John J. McNeill, this retreat became an annual event at Kirkridge and still draws large numbers to pray and share.

In his autobiography, ***Both Feet Firmly Planted in Midair: My Spiritual Journey***, John McNeill writes of how Reverend Robert Raines had read his book, ***The Church and the Homosexual***, and invited him to come to lead this new venture, but Kirkridge had been a place where questions of human sexuality and Christianity had been explored for decades. Christians discussing homosexuality was a natural evolution of the unique Kirkridge melding of Christianity with the Human Potential Movement in the early 60s.

In June, 85 Company members came to hear Gordon Cosby of Washington's Church of the Saviour discuss the difficulties of community-building. Founder of this ecumenical Christian Church devoted to service, particularly in the poorest areas of D.C., Gordon Cosby told the story of how his congregation sacrificed time, energy, and resources, inspiring the Company to once again examine their own commitment to building the Church where they lived and worked. "The Company is firmer," Jack wrote when the last member left on Sunday.

The long-awaited check from the DER for the 23-1/2 acres sold arrived on July 6. Jack used the $38,300 to pay overdue bills and loans. The checks had already been written in advance, waiting for the money to be deposited. Jack first repaid Jane $2,000 he had borrowed, and when the couple left for Chautauqua on the 15th, it was with a lighter heart.

No matter the crisis, coming to Chautauqua each summer brought happiness to Jack and Jane. Once again finding the house on the lake dirty, with yet another window broken, the couple set out to clean, repair the window, and lay new carpet in anticipation of a houseful of guests. First Berthi came to spend a few days, and immediately upon her leaving, Jack's niece Sheila, her husband and family arrived.

Before the week was over, Wenley called and asked if he could join them, and, of course, all agreed. Jack and Jane cleaned out the attic as Doug, his wife Jerry, and their son Doug ("Diggy") added to the family reunion. Noted as one of Jack's happiest summers, he and Jane came back to Kirkridge refreshed: "All Chautauqua stay great!" The remainder of the summer was spent shingling the sheep pen and trying to get Bess to find a companion.

On the 9th of September Jane left for Washington, D.C. and a Stress Without Stress weekend workshop, while Jack mourned the loss of two baby goats he purchased on Thursday but were killed by Saturday, hit by cars. Baptizing four retreatants at the Lodge on Sunday morning helped ease the sadness he felt at the loss.

Jack's memories of the September Board meeting, his first as simply a member, were painful. Having given up the directorship of Kirkridge, he might have known that the emphasis would be different, but at the executive session Jack complained that the "three-part Kirkridge motto had been omitted for a year, [there was] no Christian group under discipline, no movement for power in the Church."

Rustum Roy, "desolated" by the September 4 death of E.F. Schumacher, agreed with Jack that Kirkridge needed to find its soul once more; it had become a "Church type," not the "sect type" that Jack had envisioned three decades before. The obvious problem remained that Kirkridge was not "Jack's" in the same way it had been in the early years, and while he and Jane still lived on the property, their role had been greatly diminished–both by choice and by circumstance.

By month's end, their DER windfall down to $2,000, Jane and Jack entertained the idea of being core faculty at a proposed School of Spiritual Direction at Wainwright House in Rye, New York, a retreat center "founded in 1941 as the headquarters of the Laymen's Movement, an effort to further concepts of values and ethics in business and personal life." Yet the thought of leaving Kirkridge did not seem a viable option in the later years of this decade. Nothing is mentioned of this offer after October 3, 1977.

Jack flew to Calgary for the Naramata Centre gathering of the World Council of Churches on October 17, but came home at week's end disappointed that the conference was poor, even though he loved the city, often walking downtown and admiring the sunsets. The following week Jane flew to Banff, Alberta, Canada, for three weeks, and Jack left for Philadelphia the next day for an "Open Door" panel at First Presbyterian Church, where he spoke on "How to be Non-Violent."

He returned to Kirkridge for the Company weekend of 40 with UCC (United Church of Christ) and American Baptist Scripture scholar, Willis Elliott, keeping "low profile but did add meditation as goal." After preaching at Clinton Presbyterian on Sunday morning, Jack went back to Kirkridge for the closing of the Company weekend. "Not for me," he wrote, although for most of the Company members, the community was becoming a source of support and genuine companionship.

Jack went to the Earlham advisory meeting in mid-November, and Jane returned the week of Thanksgiving. This year the two had dinner alone, and Jack deemed it a perfect holiday. On Saturday Rick and Lori surprised them with a visit, and went to hear Jane preach in Clinton Presbyterian en route to New York the next day. On December 2 Jack and Jane attended a memorial service for a suicide victim who had once lived on the mountain, after which Jack had to dash off to the ABE airport in Allentown, Pennsylvania to attend the WANACH meeting at the Dominican House of Studies in Washington, D.C. While Jack always enjoyed these meetings, and liked J. Bryan Hehir, he wondered as he flew home to ABE, "Should I resign this group? Not yet."

With Jack chair of the nominating committee for the United Presbyterian Peace Fellowship, he and Jane went to New York City on December 7 for the annual meeting. Contending with bitter winds, Jane had to call AAA for battery problems before they could return home. The next day, battery installed, Jack went to Philadelphia for a Peace Walk. While the Vietnam War was officially over on April 30, 1975, the peace movement had not ended.

It rained on Christmas that year, Jack and Jane beginning the day with a 10:30 service at Buck Hill. Jack preached on "Stewards of Mysteries" (I Cor. 4). With his account down to 55 cents, Jack rejoiced that the TIAA $299 check arrived. As usual, the final days of the year found him writing the last of his Christmas cards.

Once again the new year began with bad weather on the mountain, but Jack and Jane drove to Princeton for the EIOS (Ecumenical Institute of Spirituality) meeting. The historical blizzard of 1978 hit home for the Nelsons. Jack memorably noted, "Never such snow and ice."

37-38.Jack and Jane Nelson shoveling snow at
Tiree (their home at Kirkridge), March 1978

Travel plans in mid-January came to a momentary halt. By the 23rd, Jack was able to fly to Alexandria for the National Peace Academy Campaign meeting. By February 6, 18-1/2 inches of snow covered the mountain, with "no let up in the freeze." Jack used the quiet time to begin tax preparation, discovering that he had given away almost $30,000 to individuals: "A crime, as Jane agreed."

What would become the most important leitmotif in 1978, however, began on February 21 when Jack noted, "Jane lymph bad." On March 2, en route to Dayton for a talk, Jack stopped by Sewickley to visit Bess, who finally told him that she was leaving $10,000 each to the four grandchildren. But this good news was balanced by Jane's continuing problems with the recurring cancer. She went to Presbyterian Hospital in Philadelphia on February 24, where they discovered a problem in her left wrist.

On March 16, Jane left for Mayo Clinic, while Jack stayed behind. The heavy schedule of travel, preaching, and leading retreats didn't let up, especially as this was the Lenten and Easter season, but when Jane called to ask him to come to Rochester, Minnesota, because they discovered a uterine tumor, he took the first plane to be with her for the hysterectomy on March 31.

Unfortunately, the surgery showed that the cancer had spread, and while he stayed at the Miller House, where Jane's sister Margaret also stayed, he left on April 3 for the Earlham School of Religion and then on to Milford, New Jersey, but phoned Jane every day, knowing that Margaret would be with her.

While Jane was recuperating, 49 Company members met at Kirkridge on April 14 for a weekend with Gregory Baum, a Roman Catholic theologian then at Canada's McGill University. Jack reflected on the direction of the Company, now two years old, and found them wanting in comparison with the Iona community in Scotland. But his disappointment, while understandable, was a bit unfair.

The community at Iona had a core group of people who lived on the island, had a set prayer and worship schedule, and followed a discipline that still had not caught on with the geographically dispersed group that met four times a year, always with an open invitation to new members, some of whom stayed, some of whom never returned. Each Company meeting began with an explanation of what the Company was and hoped to become, but for many, it was the retreat leader (such as Gregory Baum, Gordon Cosby, Douglas Steere, or Joan Chittister) who often drew new people to Kirkridge and to the Company.

Jack's hopes for what the Company could be for Kirkridge are found in his diary musings of April 16: "Can Company use Kirkridge intentions, drop Friends, have only Companions?" The reference to Kirkridge *intentions* did not mean the request for specific prayers sent in by Kirkridgers, but was a synonym for the original Kirkridge discipline or lifestyle that had been advocated in the first and second decade of Kirkridge's existence (e.g., daily prayer, use of the Kirkridge lectionary, Scripture reading, annual retreat, etc.). Those who agreed to follow this lifestyle were referred to as Friends.

The Company at Kirkridge chose the term Companions to describe themselves with the connotation of "those who share or break bread together." Jack's passion for resurrecting the Friends of Kirkridge, whatever they might be called, permeates his diary. Each Company meeting that he attended (and he was at most of the early meetings) was evaluated by this high standard, and while the newly formed group was inspired by Jack's vision and attempted to follow his original "intentions," within the first two or three years, it became evident that this new group would evolve into something unique and dedicated–but not what Jack dreamed of in 1975.

Spring of 1978 brought new turmoil into Jack's life. Hospital expenses mounted, and he borrowed $500 from Peggy, still writing of being overdrawn everywhere. Jane recovered from surgery with friends and her sister while Jack's busy schedule added a daily phone call to check on her progress.

On April 20, Jack drove hurriedly to Buffalo to meet Jane at the airport, where she arrived by wheelchair at 4:41, an hour after he arrived. As Jane's next stop was the Buffalo General Hospital, the two checked into the Holiday Inn, where they discussed divergent diagnoses and weighed treatment options. Dr. David Nichols told Jane she was healed, but suggested chemotherapy. Jane considered various non-traditional paths as well, including guided meditation, nutrition, and music.

Together the couple wandered to "wondrous" Niagara Falls on the Canadian side, a break from the fear gripping both over Jane's health. But in her vulnerable condition, she broke down upon their return from the short trip. "Argument at home," Jack wrote, "Jane's vocation at Kirkridge?" Now that she had given up the assistant directorship, with her health failing, she pondered her future and it looked bleak.

By April 23, the two were back at Kirkridge, but on the 27th Jack drove to Chautauqua, where he pruned bushes, cleaned, and called for heat to be turned on. Jane, however, courtesy of Jack's sister Peggy, stayed at Chautauqua's St. Elmo's spa since 10 North needed so much work. Jack returned to Kirkridge and called Jane, who cried for two hours, wanting to know if Jack really wanted and loved her. "I moved and helpless. Really do hold her dear," he tenderly wrote.

The next day Wenley brought his future wife, Roma, to meet Jack, and they shared a fresh strawberry pie, gift of Ruth van der Bent. On May 3 Jack drove Tom Lane to Connecticut, where Jane would be undergoing treatment at Simonton. The new dilemma was, should she combine the Simonton treatment with chemotherapy? The decisions would consume Jane for the coming months. On May 10, Jane went to the Poconos Hospital to relieve an abscess. Three days later, Jack drove her to Philadelphia Oncological Hospital to see Dr. Creech, then dashed off to give a retreat for the Somerville United Reformed group. On May 23 Jane was told that hormone therapy was all she needed. "Great news," Jack wrote. But checks continued to bounce as Jack tried to get his finances in better order.

The summer months brought more travel. Jack spent a week at the FOR Mobilization for Human Survival meeting in New York City, with Jim Wallis, Robert McAfee Brown, and friends of many decades. He was amused that his name tag read "John Oliver" as most participants called him Jack. He attended the reception hosted by his brother Doug, and learning that Jane was "bad," he sent roses.

The weekend brought 16 Princeton Crusaders together, Jack suggesting that they carry banners representing their year. Wenley and he both participated in the celebration, hindered by rain. Before the parade's conclusion, Jack hurried home to be with Jane.

On June 6 Jack drove Jane to Cornwell, Connecticut, and Phase I of the Simonton cancer treatment, but if worry about Jane weren't distracting enough, the leaking ceiling in the Tiree dining room (which Jack had covered with plastic), came crashing down with a "bang and a splash." Jack put up more plastic, as the roofer failed to show up, but Jane, now home, was comforted by women friends who sat with her, meditated with her, and made sure she had plenty of fluids, vitamin C, and nourishing foods. Two days after being at her friend Sally Bailey's ordination at Park Avenue Christian, on the 20th of June, Jane went back to Philadelphia to see Dr. Creech, then left the next day for Chautauqua with Joan Egler (and three quarts of oil for her unreliable car).

With the roof now replaced, Jack planted Jane's bulbs "in the rain," and picked her up at Chautauqua to drive with her to visit Bess in Sewickley. Jane brought chicken and good bread along, but they found Bess "feeble and alone." Jack called her doctor, got a prescription filled, and Jane fixed her hair before they drove back to Chautauqua. Happy that Bess had lent them $3,000 "until September 30" to get the roof fixed, Jack and Jane enjoyed their summer vacation, with a visit by Georgina in early August. Jane stayed at St. Elmo's once again to be near her treatment center, arriving back at Kirkridge with Georgie on the 14th. In August, shortly after the Company meeting with peace activist Al Krass, Jack discovered with a phone call to Bess that her doctor advised her going to a nursing home–but she would not hear of it.

At the September Board meeting in 1978, the Chair announced that Kresge would not give Kirkridge the $20,000 it had requested to renovate the Farmhouse, now in poor shape. The money would still have to be raised.

Jane's September appointment with Dr. Creech in Philadelphia cheered her, as her three-month checkup was good, and he gave her lots of hormone pills as part of a new treatment. This diagnosis made Jack's planned trip to the International FOR meeting in Ireland possible, and on the 14th of September, Jane drove him to Kennedy Airport. Having left his passport at home, Jane drove the 200 miles back to Kirkridge to get it, and while she made it before the plane left, Jack also left his toiletries kit on the seat of the car and had to purchase necessities when he got to Ireland.

With time to visit George MacLeod and the Iona community while in Scotland, Jack found them a "heartsome" group. He worshiped in the "chilly, damp, blessed abbey church" that he so loved, and worked on a paper for Bill Coffin by streetlight in Glasgow. He returned to New York on September 24 with Jane patiently waiting for him at the airport. "All a great dreamlike event," he wrote that evening in his diary.

On October 16 the couple finally sold their property at 94 Prospect Street in New Haven. Netting nearly $82,000 from the sale, Jane invested $20,000 at 8-1/2% on a three-month certificate. It would be the last major influx of cash the two would receive.

On November 2 Jane drove to the cancer center at Richmond, and on November 3 theologian Charles Davis was the main speaker at the Company meeting, where the group's relationship with Kirkridge was a serious subject of discussion. The Company was limited in size to perhaps 30-40 retreatants at a Company weekend. Originally intending to meet at Kirkridge four times a year, they found traveling prohibitive for many, especially in the winter months. In addition, the cost of the weekend now exceeded the fees of some other retreat centers. It was eventually decided that the group would meet twice a year a Kirkridge, and twice annually at another site. Over the years, members met at Dayspring and New Windsor Service Center in Maryland, State College, Shalom Mountain, and Mt. Saviour Monastery in Elmira, New York.

Jack's Aunt Bess fell again on the 16th, and Jack and Jane bought her a television set the following week. On the 28th Bess, feeling much better, forgave the $3,000 loan she provided for the roof, an early, much-appreciated Christmas gift. Attending the WANACH meeting in D.C. the first weekend of December, Jack was overjoyed to learn on the 5th that Jane's Philadelphia cancer checkup was fine.

While he discouraged her, Jane went off to Madison for a "healing" retreat. Trying to retrieve her health became a passion for Jane, and she not only went the medical route, she worked on diet, walked an hour a day, and sought out spiritual healing as well as medical treatment. Convinced that the cancer was in remission, Jane prepared for a small, quiet Christmas.

A young man living at Folly, the individual retreat house near the Lodge, brought them a Christmas tree and a large candle. They did not attend midnight Mass that year, but Jack shoveled snow for much of the holiday. With the trip to Ireland and Scotland still fresh in his mind, Jack sent Celtic-inspired Christmas cards this year. On New Year's Eve, he drove to Sewickley to visit Bess to celebrate her 96th birthday a few days early, and on January 2 he sent her a dozen roses to mark the day itself.

The new year of 1979 began once more in a flurry of activity. Henri Nouwen spoke at the Guild Spiritual Guidance retreat at Seabury House on January 6, and Jack drove in sleet to attend. The Eucharist in a circle on Sunday morning Jack described as "so-so," but the prayer offered "for those of us in broken stage" brought Jack to tears. Driving through snow and rain all the way home prompted Jack to write in his diary, "Worthwhile?," but he never answered the question. Arriving home he immediately immersed himself in two days of court appearances and jail visits.

39. Dan Berrigan's annual retreat at Kirkridge, January 1979

On Thursday Jack flew to Kentucky and the EIOS meeting at the Sisters of Loretto Motherhouse in Nerinx, Kentucky, where Morton Kelsey spoke on the Sociology and Psychology of Loneliness, and when Jack was driven to the nearby Gethsemane Abbey, he heard a second talk on loneliness by Jean Leclercq. He arrived home glad to see Jane once more, but within a week she left for a four-day Inner Healing Conference, and Jack experienced the loneliness they had discussed in Kentucky.

He spent the days Jane was away working on taxes, noting that he had given away over $42,000 in 1978. Rain pelted Kirkridge for two days, and the cellar at Tiree was flooded, but Jack managed to preserve the books stored there. He also used the opportunity to gather and number all his files and box them.

On February 11, Jack and Jane celebrated their 18th wedding anniversary at the Sheraton Canal Room. Jack described Jane as "hale and joyous," and the hope was that the cancer worries might be over. On March 23 Jack rejoiced at the unexpected check for $500 from the talks he had given for the Guild for Spiritual Guidance at Rye throughout February and March. The trips back and forth had been exhausting, but now that Jack no longer directed Kirkridge, these guest lectures and membership meetings gave meaning to his life.

The Kirkridge Company met in April with Rosemary Radford Ruether as discussion leader, with 23 attending. Jack concelebrated the Sunday liturgy with six other clergy. Jane Nelson, now feeling stronger, began speaking to local groups on "holistic health," a subject which she believed would be imperative in the 1980s. The couple drove to Princeton for Jack's Crusaders meeting, at which the group discussed whether to let the organization die or not.

By June the Crusaders met again, and decided not to disband yet. Jack now had been an active member for almost half a century, and over the years he continued to meet with those early cell group members. The influence of the Crusaders had much to do with the formation of Kirkridge more than thirty years earlier, and the demise of the group was not a decision to be taken lightly.

On June 9 Jack and Jane attended the cornerstone laying for Bill Cohea's chapel at Columcille. Jack wrote in his diary that he prayed the Iona prayer, a fitting choice—although he noted that he had forgotten the Kirkridge prayer. Given a clean bill of health by the Philadelphia Oncology team, Jane left for Saskatoon on June 15 to spend a few weeks with her family.

The summer of 1979 proved critical for the gasoline crisis. "Nearly all gas stations closed," Jack wrote on June 27. "None open in New York and Connecticut." Complaining that OPEC countries now raised oil to $23 a barrel (from the previous $3), Jack found gasoline at the exorbitant price of 98.9 cents a gallon, and got bus and train schedules for himself and the other mountain residents.

On July 5 Jane returned, and as Peg subsidized their annual lakeside vacation, the two drove to Chautauqua, where Jane, "weak," walked an hour a day, while Jack worked on a promised manuscript. Jane's sister Margaret joined them on the 11th but moved to the Chautauqua Inn after a few days, and Jack's niece Sheila and her children came on the 20th. Returning to Kirkridge, Jack labored over the manuscript he had been working on for months. "Slower than I recall any previous MS," he wrote in his diary."I'm getting old for sure."

As Bess needed a substitute caregiver for two weeks in August, Jack and Jane decided to offer their services. Jane helped Jack to work on the manuscript, which he described as the worst he had ever done. Finally on the 17th, he completed the 223 pages (slightly short of the 240 pages requested).

The next day he drove to Sewickley, where he found Bess very frail and in pain after her fall. Shopping for groceries when the nurse came, making meals for both of them, and staying up until 3 a.m. typing the manuscript, Jack still found time to talk to Bess about her inheritance. He encouraged her to add some of the women caregivers who had been so kind to her. She commented that a few of her "remote nephews" had no claim on her inheritance. She also wanted to give $25,000 to the Elizabeth Nelson McBride Fund for the United Presbyterian Fund for Missionaries. "Dunno," Jack wrote.

Jane arrived on the 18th to a joyful reunion. Jack drove back to Kirkridge on the 22nd and left Jane to care for Bess until Labor Day. When she returned, it became obvious that the pain Jane had been experiencing was increasing. Taking aspirin for pain in her thigh, Jane next had hip pain that the aspirin didn't alleviate. She went to a Boston cancer conference on September 21, but by month's end, Jack was still commenting on her discomfort in his diary.

In October Jack and Jane drove to the Riverside Disarmament Conference, and when they returned Jane kept her appointment with Dr. Creech at the Philadelphia Oncology. Tests did not show why she was experiencing such pain, and after Sally Bailey left, Jane tried to ease the pain with Bufferin® tablets. Jane, "weak, thin, growing wheat sprouts all over," Jack wrote in mid-November. Deciding to go to a chiropractor on the 22nd, Jane felt some relief.

A new family health crisis came when Wenley suffered two consecutive heart attacks. Jack called Peggy and Doug on November 29 to tell them of Wenley's hospitalization, but the Iran hostage crisis was commanding national attention, and Jack wrote of it in his diary for days.

The WANACH meeting in D.C. occurred on December 2. Too weary to attend Mass with the group on Sunday morning, Jack suggested that he resign from the group because of age. Nobody would listen. "Stay on," they urged, and Jack acquiesced.

Health problems dominated December, 1979. Jack came home to find Jane in even more pain, and a myelogram was ordered for the next day. Wenley, having a third heart attack, was committed to Bryn Mawr Hospital's coronary care unit, so Jack contacted the family once again. He also called Sally Bailey and Georgina Bone about Jane. The myelogram showed a pinched disk. Meanwhile, Wenley suffered a fourth heart attack, so after Jack picked Jane up from the hospital, he went to visit his brother in the evening.

On the 19th Jane called the doctor, who assured her it was a pinched disk, third vertebra, and that she should use "hot sandbags and a corset." Wenley wouldn't be home until after Christmas, so the couple decided to have Christmas as best they could. Jane, "weak and in pain," sent Jack to the Pocono Hospital for a codeine prescription, and they wrapped Christmas gifts when he returned.

Jane set the table for four on Christmas Eve, but only she and Jack had dinner together. On Christmas, however, friends gathered around the table to discuss Jane's condition, although she was bedfast all day with pain. Jack told them that the lymph nodes were cancerous. As the nodes enlarged, the pain increased from pinched nerves around the aorta. After calling Roma to inquire about Wenley, Jack told Jane of the dire prognosis.

On the 26th friends joined Jack in doing dishes and laundry all day. Jane was in less pain as she stayed in bed. Glenn and Jim Leaker arrived at 8 p.m. from Canada. Jane, drowsy from the codeine, was "up and down" for the remainder of the month. New Year's Eve, Jack wrote, was a day of giving away money. He watched the 75th anniversary of the Times Square celebration on television, and ended the year's diary with the command: "Stop giving money."

Journeys Ended, Journeys Begun

1980-1990

The new decade began on the mountain with Jane's pain lessened and Jack once again bemoaning his unfinished Christmas cards and an incomplete promised manuscript. However, a call to Peggy and Howard cheered him as he learned that Howard might conduct the St. Louis or Pittsburgh Symphonies.

But before the first week of January ended, Jane's health consumed Jack's diary entries. Jane "looks lovely but frail," he wrote, "a blessed gal." The codeine caused her almost constant nausea, but on the 8th Dr. Creech gave her a clean bill of health, prescribing a new chemotherapy drug, Tamoxifen®, as he told the couple that her lymph nodes were enlarged.

Jack's Aunt Bess fell on the 26th of January. Instead of driving to Pittsburgh, JON stayed with Jane, who felt good enough to attend a wedding on the second of February. Often "limp" from the Percocet® and Tamoxifen®, Jane also employed self-hypnosis and imaging for pain control.

She walked together with Jack, almost every day, usually driving to Lake Minsi and back. Another of the spirit-lifting activities that helped them through the winter was purchasing black and white Fritz Eichenberg prints for Kirkridge. Jack was particularly pleased with the *Christ of the Breadlines* (1953), to be hung in the dining room.

Jack never lost his love of good religious art and music, and the Eichenberg prints were among his favorites.

By mid-February they were snowbound on the mountain. Somehow, Jack managed to get to Mount Saviour for a Company gathering with Benedictine Brother David Steindl-Rast the weekend of the 23ʳᵈ. Afterwards, he drove back to State College with Rustum Roy and the artist John Freda, discussing whether Freda could draw a crowd at Kirkridge.

Jane, meanwhile, stayed with her friend Dr. Muriel McGlamery in Philadelphia. This enabled Jack to attend a peacemaking retreat when he returned to Kirkridge. An added treat was a visit from Joe Platt, 96, whose unexpected visit brought joy to the mountain. Jane returned, "radiant," on March 5, and as Sally Bailey came to visit, Jack was free on the 8ᵗʰ to drive to Sewickley to visit with Bess.

When he returned, Jane was so "drugged and groggy" that sentences had to be repeated for her. A trip to the Cancer Institute in Philadelphia and another chemotherapy shot, however, helped considerably. Jane came home feeling much better. She sent flowers to Muriel to thank her for the extended stay, where the two had flown kites together. But the euphoria didn't last.

On March 23 Jane discovered that she had phlebitis in her left leg, and the heavy pain medication began again. Three days later, Jack and Jane discussed whether she should spend a month's vacation in Saskatoon with her family. Instead, she went to visit with Muriel again shortly after Easter.

With Jane away, Jack gave a retreat at Manchester College on vocation and peace. He called Bess from the airport, but she said not to visit. Instead he came back to Kirkridge to discover that someone had robbed them while both were gone. Jane's car and typewriter were stolen, along with the television he had bought for her and an attaché case. The recreation room door had been broken. Jane returned home "desolate" when she discovered what had happened.

The couple celebrated her birthday with brunch at the Sheraton, and Wenley, who sent her white daisies, insisted that Jane should stay with them while Jack was away. However, she was more comfortable staying with women friends.

Jack, in the meantime, was feeling guilty for not being a better caregiver. His April 20 entry reads: "Aware of God's displeasure at my putting off tasks and MSS[manuscripts]." Adding to the problems of the week, he got a call from Howard that Peg had fallen and hit her head. He drove to Rochester to visit her, staying only overnight so as not to leave Jane long alone. "Jane does need more of my presence and affection," he wrote, and the next day the two purchased a '74 maroon Plymouth to replace her stolen car and a new typewriter at the office supply store. "Overdrew all my accounts," he added.

On April 25 Jack drove to Dayspring for a Seekers retreat, where he revised the interview for *Faith at Work*. Receiving $125 for the retreat, he deducted the cost of gas at $50, and decided he made only about $15 a talk. But Manchester College sent him $250 plus travel costs for that retreat, and this check helped his finances for the week. In early May Jane's pain seemed to have subsided, so they decided that he could go back to Dayspring for the second Seekers retreat, yet he wrote in his diary upon his return: "All that travel for 12 retreatants, leaving Jane alone," and on May 7 he drove Jane back to Muriel's

40. Jane Bone Nelson, May 1980

41. Dayspring Retreat led by Jack Nelson on May 3, 1980

The Company met at Kirkridge the weekend of May 9. Gordon Cosby of Church of the Saviour led the weekend. Jack also attended the Board meeting that weekend, where Bob told of a deficit.

On Sunday morning, Jack left the Company to preach at Hazleton, and on Tuesday he drove to Princeton, where he led the memorial service for his classmates of 1930. Jack called Jane daily. He drove to Philadelphia from Princeton to pick her up, along with a birthday cake that Muriel had baked for his 71st birthday. The next day Ruth brought a second apple birthday cake for their dessert. Jack left for the Wainwright meeting in Rye on spirituality and debated whether it should be his last. It would not be.

By June 4 Jane was back at Muriel's and not doing well. As Muriel went to Oklahoma for a reunion, Jane checked herself into the Oncologic Center. Jack called Bess, 97, who told him she was miserable, and now in a wheelchair—so Jack went back down to Pittsburgh to visit with her. He found her gloomy, having had a mild stroke the week before. As usual, he prayed with her before driving back to Kirkridge.

On June 12, Jack drove to get Jane, whose test results showed that she had lost the use of one kidney. Not discouraged, Jane was tired but newly eager to battle the health problems that now were daily. Jack received the $3,780 final payment on the 1977 land deal, plus some money from a stock sale that week, so a few more bills could be paid. The two went to Poplar Valley Methodist together on the 22nd, but by July 1 Jane was confined to bed. Her sister Margaret came from Canada to care for her, and within the week both of them drove to Philadelphia to be with Muriel.

July 11 marked the departure day for Jack to head for Chautauqua and prepare the house for the annual summer vacation. Since neither would be home, he took the new television and typewriter with him to State College, where he had a picnic with Company members at the weekend meeting. On Sunday morning Jack left early to drive to Sewickley to visit Bess, whom he found "plaintive and crying." After spending one and a half hours with her, Jack left for Chautauqua. Again, finding the place an incredible mess, he hired some help to clean, while he put up the screens and prepared the grounds around the house in preparation for Jane's arrival with Margaret and Muriel.

While Margaret attended ***Carmen*** with a friend of Jack's, he and Jane and Muriel sat around the kitchen table discussing how seriously she needed his support. And he tried, preparing soup for everyone each day. When Jane ran out of her medication, Jack spent a day trying to find it locally, then drove almost back to Kirkridge to get it from a hospital pharmacy.

Jane's sister Ella came to join her and Margaret, and while Jane was experiencing great pain, having her sisters near her always brought comfort. On the 24th Jack drove Jane to St. Luke's for her chemotherapy. When he came back to Chautauqua, Ella and Margaret had cleared and cleaned everything, to the couple's delight.

42. Jack and Jane Nelson, Margaret Bone
Leaker, and Ella Bone in July 1980

After Jane and her sisters retired for the night, Jack re-read his diaries from 1977 and '78. Noting that many of the names reoccurred in his diaries, he reflected: "All too short a time here!"—but whether he meant on earth or at Chautauqua, only JON would know. With Jane in pain and resting for much of the day, her sisters cleaned out and papered kitchen shelves, while Jack pulled weeds, cut back vines, and trimmed hedges.

But the days at Chautauqua were also filled with morning services, afternoon lectures, choral practice, and evening entertainment. Margaret and he saw a "perfect" *Magic Flute* and *Midsummer Night's Dream* earlier in the month. Even with Jane's illness, the few weeks spent on the lake were an idyll, but on August 4, all left the cottage and Jack visited Bess before driving back to Kirkridge.

As Margaret still remained with Jane, Jack drove to State College to discuss a project. He sought to have some of the Fritz Eichenberg woodcut prints, from the Catholic Worker, that hung in many of the bedrooms at Kirkridge enlarged and mounted on poster board. A much more complicated process than it would be today, this project became a joint effort of Jack, Rustum Roy, and Cal Garber, a Board member who worked at Kodak and took charge of enlarging the first of the engravings, *Christ of the Breadlines*. Jack even took the enlarged print to Rhode Island for Fritz Eichenberg to see, and the artist was pleased at the different effect of the enlargement.

That same Sunday Jack, Bob Raines, and the Institutional Development Committee met to discuss a cemetery at Kirkridge, which today is the memorial garden in front of Turning Point, with a Celtic cross similar to the one at Iona overlooking the hill. With 5,000 now on the mailing list, the group discussed the need for a dedicated group of Kirkridgers who could be a continued source of revenue.

By this time the Company at Kirkridge was meeting on the mountain only once or twice yearly. While the group was cohesive and supportive of each other, they were not the "third order" that Jack had envisioned in 1975 who would embody the discipline that marked the earliest Kirkridgers. Yet for the remainder of his life, Jack tried to attend each Company meeting, providing inspiration and a link to Kirkridge's roots.

On August 14 Jack drove Jane to Philadelphia for chemotherapy, and on the way home stopped for her hypnosis treatment. Having decided against acupuncture, Jane chose to try hypnosis to help with pain control. That night, Jack wrote that he ate his "standup supper" alone. Jane couldn't eat, was lonely, and rejoiced that Georgina came to stay with her that weekend.

On the 22nd Jack wrote to Rick, telling him about Jane's condition. A week to the day he showed up for a visit, helping Jack to put a new deck on Tiree. Though he left on September 2, he and Jack had long talks about Jane and the future. Since Georgina had to leave on August 25, after Rick left Kirkridge, Jane went to stay with Muriel again.

43. Sexuality Workshop on August 24, 1980. Participants
in photo include Muriel McGlamery, M.D., JON, an
unidentified participant, Della Roy, Rustum Roy,
Anne Stewart, Jane Nelson, and Georgina Bone.

While Jack was concerned about the health problems of Jane and
Bess, not to mention Peggy and Wenley, he still preached on many
Sundays, gave retreats, taught occasional classes at the Earlham
School of Religion, attended meetings of numerous groups, and
continued to care about the future of Kirkridge. On September 4,
Jack hung fifteen Eichenberg prints in various Kirkridge buildings,
but not yet the enlarged print of *Christ of the Breadlines* on display in
the dining room. (For the 50th anniversary of Kirkridge in 1992, this
print was used for the poster.) At the September 13 Board meeting
Jack and Rustum agreed to get a price on five or six 8 x 10 Eichenberg
prints, and Jack promised to contribute $500 over the coming year to
help defray the Kirkridge debt.

By month's end, Jack gave a retreat at Kirkridge for the Branford Congregation. Although undergoing radiation almost daily, and often in great pain, Jane felt well enough to serve tea at Tiree for the 16 retreatants. Another joy for Jane was Georgina's doctoral graduation from the University of Alberta on September 26. As a gift, Jane and Jack purchased Georgina's graduation hood, worn during the Ph.D. commencement ceremony.

Harvey Cox led the Company weekend on "Liberation and Spirituality" for 50 participants the weekend of October 10-12. Jack noted in his diary that the Kirkridge prayer book and hymnal were "beat up," and he decided that a worthwhile project might be to replace both of them, a project that he took up with the Company and the Sycamore Community—and both projects were completed before his death.

Jane was now taking the nutritional liquid supplement Ensure® since eating had become so difficult for her, and she decided against hospice, although she and Jack discussed the possibility. On most days, she needed pain injections every two hours. On the 17th Jack learned that he could get $7,000 per acre by selling part of the land, and he and Jane decided to consider it. On the 20th, Jane cashed in her Treasury bonds to help with the expenses, and Jack paid all the bills except what he owed her, sending $2,000 to Rick at her request.

Jane, weak and often nauseated, was now getting radiation almost daily, and Jack made sure that she had someone to care for her while he went off to Harper's Ferry for the Trail Ministry of the Synod. Halloween weekend, the Berrigans gave a retreat at Quiet Ways, and Jack discussed the coming Presidential election with them. Jane's doctor told her on November 3 that she was making progress, and that eliminating certain foods should prevent nausea. On the 6th of November, Jack finally could put up the striking Eichenberg *Christ of the Breadlines* print in the Turning Point dining room. Two days later he flew to the Earlham School Board meeting.

With a respite from the radiation, Jane walked with Jack in the dark around Lake Minsi on November 13, leaving for Toronto and Saskatoon four days later. Air Canada had a wheelchair ready for her. When she returned from visiting her family two weeks later, she was strengthened and her pain was considerably relieved. On December 3, Jane was back with Muriel, and Jack drove to the Dominican House of Studies for the annual WANACH meeting. Three days later Jane's friend, Martha, stayed with her while Jack went to his FOR meeting at Nyack. The meeting was led by Dom Helder Camara, a Catholic archbishop of Recife, Brazil, who honored and remembered Dorothy Day. Dorothy's death on December 4 saddened all at the meeting, as well as those she helped through the Catholic Worker Movement (CWM).

The following week Jane's stolen car was found, and the person suspected of stealing it had the owner's card with him. It turned out to be one of the young men whom Jack had befriended. With Jane gaining strength, Jack purchased 400 Christmas cards on December 17, but that evening, the call came from Pittsburgh that his Aunt Bess had died, and Jack flew to Pittsburgh the next morning to make arrangements for a later funeral. Luckily, Georgina had planned to come to Kirkridge to spend Christmas with the couple, and while Jane was "weak and wan," Jack decorated Tiree with a small tree and lit candles for a festive atmosphere.

On New Year's Day, 1981, Jack, the prolific card sender, tried to decide if they should send any cards that year. Jack was invited to a New Year's gathering at the van der Bents, leaving Jane and Georgina alone. Hearing a thump in the bedroom, Georgina rushed to Jane's side as Jack returned to the house. In the midst of a blizzard, the ambulance Jack called could not drive up to the front of house. The emergency attendants carried Jane on a stretcher to the ambulance and on to St. Luke's ICU. Jack and Georgina followed over treacherous roads.

With Georgina having to return to Canada, Jack stayed all the next day as Jane had surgery to suture ruptured vessels. Muriel took a room at a hotel near the hospital to be near her. Jack spent January 3 washing sheets, cleaning the house, and taking down the tree and all Christmas decorations.

As Jane's sutures were holding, she told Jack, "I'll walk out of here." The doctor gave them both hope that she was progressing and could come home soon. Jack spent much of the week writing the *Ridgeleaf,* calling his family, planning the memorial for Bess, and writing her history for the eulogy. With a five-inch snowfall, Jack asked Bob Bankes to plow so that cars could get in and out. Cindy Raines and the van der Bents provided meals—yet no cards were sent that Christmas.

As he was trying to work on two manuscripts and the memorial service, Jack discovered to his dismay on December 8 that the thief had also stolen the Nelson family sterling silver set. The next day after contacting the police about the theft, he obtained $116,000 in stock certificates and put them "pronto" into a safe deposit box with other stock certificates. On Sunday, January 11, he visited Jane and flew to Pittsburgh for Bess's memorial, where he wore his blue Yale robes. Thirty-six attended the service. Jack flew back immediately, and for the first time he wrote in his diary that he and Jane discussed her possible death and what her wishes were concerning the arrangements.

Meanwhile on the mountain, Jack interspersed visits to Jane with work on a manuscript that was due, and providing "taxi service" for those who needed rides and had no transportation. He attended the East Bangor Ministerium meeting on the 14th and the following day the Institute of Spirituality meeting at Marriottsville. At each gathering, all prayed for Jane. On the 16th Jack drove to the Carmelite Monastery in Baltimore for another EIOS meeting, and when he returned home the next day, he saw Sally Bailey's car and knew that Jane was home from St. Luke's. Since Pat Bland from Victoria came to stay with Jane, Jack went back to Baltimore for the remainder of the meeting.

On the 21st the couple made arrangements for a visiting nurse to come to Tiree. Jack called Peg, who had just had surgery for breast cancer. By Sunday the 25th, Jane was able to join him for a meal at the table, but the pain had now gone from her leg to her whole torso, and she was once again on the pain medication. After the two prayed together that night, Jane told Jack that her ministry now was "with those who call and write."

On February 5, Jack and Jane once again discussed her death, and she made a will modeled on Bess's. Jack borrowed another $1,000 from her to pay the hospital bill, and now owed her $7,400. With Bess gone and Jane dying, his siblings became a new worry for Jack. Two calls on Saturday the 7th prompted him to write: "WDN [Wenley] low, Peg down"—but both would outlive Jack. On the 9th Jack drove to Yale, then spent a few days at Bess's, writing up an inventory of her belongings. He offered Jane her $1,000 engagement ring, but Jane said she "preferred zircon."

For Valentine's Day Jack took Jane and Patty, who had been staying with her, to the Bartonsville Holiday Inn for a 20th anniversary dinner. The next day he drove Patty to the airport, and that week he and Bill Cohea drove to Sewickley for a third haul of the items he wanted to bring to Tiree from Bess's.

On February 26th Jack got the call that Peg's husband, Howard Hanson, internationally known composer and Director of the Eastman School of Music for 40 years, had died at 85. Jack drove to the funeral in Rochester on March 3, a "glorious affair with 23 trombones." The next day he met with Peg and Doug about getting a new lawyer and power of attorney to help with trusts and other legal matters. He drove home on the 5th to spend the day in support court with men he had been helping.

With her sister Margaret staying with her, Jane was "lovely and conversational" when he returned from the funeral. He drove to

Mount Saviour in Elmira for the Company weekend with Benedictine monk Sebastian Moore, writing that he had to stop at rest stops to sleep on the way home. The morning after he returned, Jane had to be taken to St. Luke's, where the doctor told her that the cancer that had overtaken her body had been latent since her 1956 mastectomy. Jack took advantage of Margaret's presence to gather and sell Bess's jewelry. He used $800 of the thousand he received to pay bills, then worked until 3:30 in the morning typing a symposium paper on psychology and religion.

On March 20 the long-awaited check from Bess's estate arrived, and he repaid Jane all the money he owed her, putting the rest in the bank. Six days later he drove Margaret to the airport. That Sunday Jane was well enough to accompany him to a Knights of Columbus spaghetti dinner on the 29th. Jack celebrated the fourteenth anniversary of the AA group at Kirkridge that Sunday as well. Two days later, U.S. President Ronald Reagan survived an assassination attempt.

Jane felt strong enough to take a short walk around Lake Minsi with Jack on April 1. A few days later a check arrived for Jack as executor of Bess's estate, and he made arrangements for $5,000 to be sent to the Presbytery as she requested. While Jane asked him "urgently" not to go anywhere, Jack nonetheless took a few more of the McBride estate items to Philadelphia for appraisal "to stay alive." On March 8 Roma called, hoping Jack would come to visit Wenley, but he called him instead, and took Jane to St. Luke's for another kidney scan.

By the 11th, Jane was undergoing radiation again, and Muriel "blessedly" came to be with her for a few hours. On the 15th Jane was back in the hospital, but "very normal and conversational." Learning of her illness, Henri Nouwen sent a wire to both Jack and Jane. The two agreed to sell lots on Route 191 to help with finances. With Jane in the hospital, Jack took a lamp, crystal, and jewelry from the estate for appraisal, coming home with $600. "Can stop taking cash from Jane," he wrote.

On the 22nd Jane's doctors proposed hypophysectomy, the surgical removal of the pituitary gland, but she said no surgery—asking instead for lipstick and her blue robe. Jack called Georgina, Wenley, and Peg, and on the 24th Jane called him and asked him to "come and talk."

Five days later Tsuneo, the Asian gentleman suspected of being the one who later returned to visit Jack's grave, called to tell Jack that he'd be coming to Kirkridge on June 17 for the tenth reunion of SAKI students, so Jack cleaned a room in preparation for the unexpected visit. By month's end, Jane was on a liquid diet but was brighter. Her weight went up from 94 to 98 lbs., and with the weight gain her spirits rose. By May 4 she weighed 108 lbs., and when Georgina called and told her to come home to Canada, she told Jack cheerily, "I'll fly Friday."

On May 8 Jane left the hospital, and Jack took her directly to the airport where a wheelchair awaited her. She flew from Buffalo to Toronto and on to Saskatoon to be with her family, the trip a gift from Georgina. Immediately upon her arrival, her sisters tried to get her an appointment at the pain clinic there. When Jack called her, he discovered she was in good spirits and sounded "hale." Her appointment was set for May 14, Jack's 72nd birthday.

On the Monday after Jane left, Jack discovered that checks had been stolen and cashed, a prelude to what would become a series of robberies at Kirkridge for the remainder of the decade. Jack celebrated his birthday with the van der Bents, and his call to Jane that night revealed that she would begin chemo again on the 15th. Her new physician, Dr. Shapiro, thought chemotherapy every three weeks was in order, as he found a nodule in her neck. Jane seemed calm about the treatment when he called her the day after treatment began.

With Jane away, Jack reverted to his usual activity. Plans for a SAKI reunion absorbed his time. He interviewed candidates for the

Presbytery, drove to Philadelphia for a Prison Society talk, finished a review of *A Just Peace* for the FOR, and sent a copy of the review with his letter to Jane. Now down to 99 lbs., Jane had a persistent abdominal pain, but she remained hopeful and cheerful when she called. Believing she'd be returning soon, Jack dug out a tomato and lettuce garden and planted 20 tomato plants, placing a wire fence around it for protection.

On May 30 Georgina notified Jack that Jane's leg was greatly swollen, she had blood clots, and the chemo caused hair loss, but Jack gave no indication in his diary that he planned a trip to Canada. Still selling items he brought from Bess's, his diary entry for June 1 notes with some surprise that a silver serving plate he had given the family in 1930 brought $117 half a century later.

A call to Margaret Leaker the next day informed Jack that while Jane's leg was still swollen, she was on Heparin® and that alleviated the swelling. Still Jack never made arrangements to be with her, although he sent letters and forwarded her mail. On June 11 Margaret called again to tell him that a new cancer in the abdomen was diagnosed, and the second chemotherapy she had undergone was painful. "She wants my voice, alas!" he wrote.

From June 12 to 14 Jack participated in the Gay and Christian retreat at Kirkridge, led by Beverly Harrison and Carter Heywood. He also remodeled the kitchen downstairs with new cabinets and appliances, something that Jane had wanted him to do. This gave work to some of the men that he had helped financially over the years.

On June 14, he preached a Trinity Sunday sermon at Water Gap, had dinner with friends at Howard Johnson's, and was in bed by 2:00. At 4:15 Georgina called: "Jane bleeds, is sinking, down to 112 lbs., wants an operation, but Drs. Shapiro and Burton don't know where…." Jack's diary entry for June 15 reads simply: "At 7:30 our time Jane's heart did stop, Cohea and Raines in by 8."

Getting the first flight he could, Jack stayed with Lloyd's family. He ordered flowers, signed for an autopsy ("an aorto-enthric fistula took her"), bought a mahogany box for her ashes, and wrote a biography for the obituary and funeral. Dr. Burton told Jack that at 4:30 the morning Jane died, she said, "The sun's coming up bright," and her last words were, "Oh, that's nice."

Her funeral at the Grosvenor Park United Church on June 17 at 1:30 had six honorary pallbearers and four speakers, with Jack's comments last. He concluded his eulogy at her funeral: "Jane McTaggert Bone Nelson silently – and to the end – bravely and buoyantly – slipped off to be more fully in the kingdom which she had served with all her energies over the years." Later that night in his journal, he wrote "Many loved her." For years after Jane died, he always told Company members that his 20 years with Jane were the happiest of his life, and those who knew him well all agreed.

Years later his niece and Jane's sisters still pondered Jack's hesitancy to fly to Canada to be with Jane at the end, but the general opinion seems to be that he had refused to believe that she was actually going to die, thus the garden and remodeled kitchen. That inability to believe that death was imminent would recur with his own last days nine years later.

Jane's family met for breakfast at Lloyd's the morning after the funeral and discussed "complex, international bequest items," but Jack doesn't name them. He returned to Pennsylvania after lunch with the mahogany urn in a yellow zippered bag. Now back at Kirkridge with Jane gone, Jack had the SAKI tenth reunion before him. Tsuneo and Tosheo arrived on the 19th, along with 23 other alumni, and Jack wrote that Stephanie Johnson "moved [him] to tears" when she played Brahms *Intermezzo* on the piano at Tiree. "Many called, little done," he wrote that night.

Jack took the visiting couple to Blakeslee White Haven Children's Day, where he preached at the morning service. Bill Cohea visited Jack late that evening for a quiet talk. "I have no plans," he wrote. But on Monday, Tsuneo and Tosheo drove to D.C., and Bob and Cindy asked Jack to help plan a Kirkridge memorial for Jane. Dozens of cards and calls continued to come, but with Jane gone, Jack's diary once again reverted to entries of handouts to the many who saw Jack as their local bank and unemployment office.

On Wednesday Tsuneo and Tosheo came back to Tiree, where Jack had prepared dinner for them, but as they had stopped to eat on the way, Jack "unset the table and unhappily ate alone." Rick arrived from Honomu on Thursday for the memorial service to be held Saturday afternoon at 2:30 in the Lodge. The service consisted of readings from Scripture, Henri Nouwen's note to Jack and Jane in her illness, bagpipes, the singing of Jack's favorite hymn, "Be Thou My Vision," tributes, and Rusty's "good closing prayer." Doug, Rick, Georgina and Dan Berrigan attended, along with many friends.

With the service for Jane over, on Sunday morning Rick and Jack went to the Lower Valley Friends meeting where Jack spoke. The two then had brunch with Bill Cohea and Fred Lindkvist, while Georgina went through Jane's letters and photos. For the next few days, Georgina "pored over everything in Jane's room" before flying back to Saskatoon.

Rick took only a few things with him from Jane's effects, including "odd cups" and a diamond pin for Lori, but "no cash." He just made the United flight home to Hawaii. With Rick safely on his way, Jack drove in the rain to Rochester to visit with his recently widowed sister. "Had fine talk with frail, stoop[ed] and clear-minded Peg," he wrote. Next morning Jack and Peggy went to the bank, where she gave Jack $140 "for expenses," and after breakfast he took off to Chautauqua to prepare for a vacation without Jane for the first time in twenty years.

As usual, Jack threw himself into cleaning the summer home, enlisting local help in the effort. With the dryer broken, Jack washed more than a dozen dirty towels he discovered and hung them to dry. Within 48 hours he was back on the road to Stroudsburg and found the needy waiting at his door. The $140 was gone by the weekend—and he lent Jane's car to one of them "till 12."

Jack went to Buck Hill on Sunday, leading 35 "shepherdless" Quakers. He came home to begin writing thank you notes for the many cards, calls, and flowers sent after Jane's death—while the car was still not returned as promised. Wenley and Roma hoped Jack would join them in Nantucket, but he needed to stay home long enough to settle unpaid taxes and other bills and finish the thank you notes.

Jack was heartened by a call from Peg, but there was no further offer of money. Two days later, however, she took pity and said she'd send additional cash. "Bless her," he wrote. Part of his gratitude reflected the fact that he had given away $325 to various supplicants—and put up $5,000 bail for one of the men he helped who'd been arrested for burglary. At least Jane's car had been returned after three days. Jack also contacted Jane's sister Margaret, although late in the evening, and noted that he did not want to lose contact with the Bone family.

By the weekend Jack drove to State College for the annual Arts Festival. Restless, Jack headed back to Kirkridge after lunch with the Roys on Sunday. On Monday morning Jack wrote, "First day I didn't make my bed. Why should I?" But his spirits rose when Peg's $400 check arrived. Jack sent it immediately to cover checks he had written. He also rejoiced that Bess's lamp netted $513.50.

Jack left Thursday for Chautauqua and was gladdened to meet old friends at the gate upon his arrival. His days there were filled with prayer services, choir practice, concerts, teas, and *Rigoletto* with Roberta Peters' "amazing voice." As the days went on, he continued to clean out drawers at the house, get thank you notes mailed, and purchase clothing and bedding from the Jamestown Salvation Army. Jack played the classical music station, WNEB, as background while in the house, and the music provided solace.

On July 27 he invited a motet choir to 10 North and served doughnuts and coffee for a morning concert. The next day he laid out a lunch of cucumber, tuna, and ham sandwiches for twelve, inviting some of his friends and acquaintances to spend a leisurely afternoon of conversation. One guest praised his *Contours, Ridgeleaf,* and books. "Why not preach at Shadyside [Presbyterian]?" he was asked, but Jack didn't promise. That evening he returned to the now empty house in Chautauqua and wrote 31 more cards until 2 a.m. "I alone," he wrote.

But the aloneness ended when Peg and a driver arrived at 10 North at 1 a.m. the following day. Jack's friend, from Chautauqua, took the driver to the airport the next day, leaving Jack and Peg, both recently widowed, to share the house on the lake. Unfortunately, old family arguments surfaced, and Jack decided to cut his stay short and head back to Kirkridge where stacks of mail awaited him. Finding two windows had been pried, Jack discovered $35 was also missing, and within a few days he learned that once again it had been taken by one of the men who appeared regularly at his door asking for money.

The first weekend of August Jack drove to State College for a Company weekend on the topic of science and religion led by Rustum Roy. The companionship he felt from the Company did not take away his loneliness, but it was a temporary and needed reprieve.

Margaret Leaker informed Jack that he owed $1100 for Jane's funeral, and the sale of 100 Gulf shares at $41 allowed this and other bills to be paid. But the giving continued as well. One of the men who benefited from Jack's largesse met him at the bank in Stroudsburg, took $35 he needed for court, and ran out the door without a thank you. When Jack went to the Public Defender's office, the man had neither shown up nor called, and he realized with dismay that once again his trust had been misplaced. Always believing the best in others had cost Jack dearly over the years.

The lazy days of August filled with sun and breezes lifted Jack's spirits. He got bids on remodeling the recreation room, participated in a forum at Lock Haven State on Soviet-American relations, and preached on Bread for the World at Portland on the last Sunday of the month. Days were now filled with remodeling and construction, transforming Tiree's lower floor into recreation and storage room areas. On August 28, he wrote: "Burned a whole heap of Jane's files and letters," a great loss to the history of Jack Nelson and Kirkridge, not to mention Jane's history.

As August turned to September Jack's life and diary were once again filled with notations of his generosity. A motorcycle for one—and payment of the fine when the driver was stopped with no license. Two others got their used cars back in running condition—all on Jane's "blest insurance," he noted, and one wonders if Jane would have gladly advised Jack to use the money in this manner. A few women asked for money for school clothes for their children and got it, but "no to Montessori!"

On the 8th of September, Jack once again "ruthlessly" cleaned out more of Jane's files. "I must be sure to clean out my files!" he wrote in the diary, but how much pruning Jack actually accomplished is a mystery.

With Jane gone, friends and colleagues encouraged Jack to take on projects. A card from Rustum suggests for JON to write the story of the Company, "astonishingly accurate and typically lyrical." This never materialized, nor did Rustum's plea to "get the Kirkridge and *Contours* story out." Sitting still long enough to produce a finished manuscript was often low on Jack's list of priorities, even though he was undoubtedly the "lyrical" author that Rustum's note described.

On September 14, Jack finally decided to take up Wenley's offer to visit at Nantucket. En route, he delivered Jane's treasured 13-volume ***Interpreter's Bible*** and a few items of clothing to her close friend, Sally Bailey. The three days Jack spent on Nantucket began with a "storm-blasting Nor'easter" and generally bad weather, but he enjoyed reminiscing with his elder brother. "O, the life of retired leisure," Jack wrote. "Nantucket a stormy idyll amid lotus eaters." Reflecting on why he would not join his brother and live on Nantucket permanently, he wrote: "All too rich and urbane for me, dull landscape, arty or cocktaily people. I'd go up the wall there."

Jack returned to Kirkridge just long enough to pack for a flight to a Friends meeting at Indianapolis. He gave two talks on vocation and deepening worship, almost missed the return flight Sunday evening, but decided it was a worthwhile mission, especially the weekend's emphasis on peacemaking.

The following weekend he led a retreat at Turning Point for the Branford group. At 1:30 a.m. Thursday morning Jack was roused by a call from Bill Cohea, who lived at the foot of the Kirkridge property, telling Jack that an ambulance and many red lights were on Fox Gap Road, and a car was being hoisted out of a ravine. Jack went down to discover that the car was one of his donated automobiles. The driver had been pistol-whipped by two hitchhikers, angry that he had nothing to take. Seriously injured, the young man was taken to Poconos Hospital where Jack stayed with him until his sister arrived.

With another retreat at New Canaan Presbyterian Church on the topic, "What Makes a Nation Strong and Secure?" Jack enjoyed the circle of 23 retreatants discussing US-Soviet relations from a Christian perspective. With forty years of peacemaking efforts behind him, Jack to the end of his life tried to help others understand the causes and costs of war and the Christian call to a just peace.

"Despite all my vows, giveaway programs continue," Jack wrote on October 7. A camera, a water pump, a rent payment, an unpaid VA hospital bill, and a $200 freezer for Kirkridge—Jack's diary contains a laundry list of requests seldom denied. As men poured cement for the porch at Tiree, Jack noted that the workers would demand $1,300 as soon as the work was done, and he had only $200 in his account. So once again, Jack sold shares of his Gulf stock, which along with

Jane's insurance paid the bill for blacktopping the road and pouring the cement porch.

The Company at Kirkridge returned to the mountain the weekend of October 9-11. Quaker Douglas Steere of Haverford and his wife Dorothy attracted a large group of retreatants for the event. Part of the weekend was devoted to small-group discussions with Company members about the growing tension with Kirkridge over communication, cost, and commitment to the original vision for both Kirkridge and also the Company. By the end of the decade the group ceased holding meetings on the mountain that had inspired Jack and the early Kirkridgers.

Jack continued to travel for the rest of October, preaching at Weatherly and driving to Highacre House in Harper's Ferry for a meeting paid for by the Synod. Before month's end, Jack accidentally cut his hand on one of the thermo-pane windows and had to get a splint for it, but even being "one-handed" didn't slow the pace.

He visited Wenley the last weekend of October, and after stopping at the Bryn Mawr Hospital to get the bandage changed on his hand, he visited Woodlynde School, in Strafford, Pennsylvania, where he spoke on peacemaking, as rooted in the New Testament. Hearing that his TGS (Trans Gas Del Sur) stock split, making him $116,000 richer, helped ease the pain of the injured hand. One of the first things he did with his newfound wealth was to pay for someone's trip to Florida (even giving him a small suitcase that had belonged to his mother) where the man believed a job and new future awaited—it didn't, as a collect call the next week disclosed. Jack also bought tools at Sears for another at the cost of $715.

A board meeting for the Earlham School of Religion in Richmond, Indiana, the first weekend of November was marred only by the pain in his hand. He went to the hospital and had the dressing changed and received a prescription for an antibiotic as the hand became infected. Upon returning home, Jack began work on the next *Ridgeleaf,* and bemoaned the fact that the $1,000 he had asked his accountant to send was almost gone.

Jack drove to Peg's for Thanksgiving, and she was pleased with the photographs of Josiah Dodds that he gave to her. Despite her pleas, Jack drove back that evening to Kirkridge, only to find that while he was gone someone had broken into the house and stolen paintings from the wall, damaging the sash in the newly remodeled recreation room. Eric Pareis suggested Jack get a burglar alarm. But by the time Jack finally left Kirkridge later in the decade, there was little left of any value in the house, much if not all of it stolen by men he helped with money, cars, and job prospects.

Jack drove to his WANACH meeting in Washington the first weekend of December. He came home to discover he was overdrawn by almost $300, so he called for more stock dividends to be sent. Deciding to go to Peg's for Christmas, Jack reflected on December 13 about how much money he had given away; "gyped a lot!" he noted. He put up a few lights for the holiday season, got $5,000 from his broker to catch up on unpaid bills and an alarm system, and wrote a few cards.

On Christmas Eve he drove to Wenley's for a short visit, drove to his nephew John's for an even briefer visit, and then spent some time with Peg, but after dinner on Christmas day he sped back home (getting another speeding ticket), and that evening he called Lloyd Bone. The year ended with more preaching at local churches, the last of the therapy sessions on his injured hand, and a long list of beggars at the door. A few now shared the house, but none permanently. The journals ended in 1981. Most likely they were lost in the transfer of his papers, but the day-to-day notations ended with December 31, 1981.

Left without Jane to anchor him, Jack tried to maintain his hectic schedule of preaching, visiting prisoners, writing for Kirkridge publications, joining the Company at Kirkridge for weekend meetings, going to Chautauqua in summers, and keeping in touch with friends and family across the country. When Jane died, Jack's three siblings were all alive, although in varying degrees of ill health. He lived at Kirkridge for most of the decade. After he discontinued driving long distances, friends ferried him to speaking engagements, to his sister Peggy's for holidays, and into Bangor and Stroudsburg for banking and shopping. Eric Pareis, a friend and driver of the later years, recounted how Jack never lost his love of fast food, and they often stopped in their travels at a McDonald's® or Burger King® for a welcome meal. Both the taste and the cost pleased him.

In 1982 Kirkridge celebrated its 40th anniversary, and in May of the following year Jack went with twenty other Kirkridgers to Iona to explore their Celtic roots. The following year he led a July retreat for the Rolling Ridge Community to dialogue with them and evaluate their development plans. Northampton County Area Community College, with which Jack had been affiliated for most of his Kirkridge years, asked him to lecture in April on "The Purpose of Retirement," for their Older Adult Program. In November of that year he attended a fetal alcohol syndrome conference at the same college, sponsored by the Bethlehem Council of Alcoholism and Alcohol Abuse, an organization he was active in for more than a decade. On October 13, 1985, Jack served as guest pastor at the Faith United Presbyterian Church, Pen Argyl, Pennsylvania. He chose "How to Recognize Royalty" as his sermon topic. Jack remained active in the Bangor Area Ministerium until 1987.

Sir George MacLeod, 92, welcomed Jack and 32 other pilgrims to Iona in 1987, Jack's last major trip. As the years passed, the tension between Jack and the Kirkridge administration and Board grew. Philanthropic profligacy continued as Jack's funds dwindled. The ne'er-do-wells who had made demands on him for years continued to plead for rent money, alimony, car repair and doctor bills, and Jack tried to help when he could.

In 1988 Jack traveled to Rhode Island at the invitation of his niece Sheila's husband, Rev. Leo Hourihan, to speak at a statewide Prayer for Christian Unity. Ever-trusting, Jack arranged with a couple of the less-than-honorable men he knew to deliver him to a train or bus to Providence. The drivers hit him, bloodied his nose, and stole his wallet. Somehow he still managed to get to New Haven, where his brother Doug picked him up at the station, gave him money and a meal, and got him onto a train to Providence.

Doug tried to get Jack to call Leo to tell him he couldn't make it. But since Jack had given his word, he would not reconsider. Although he arrived with blood stains on his blazer, Jack got through the service and headed back to Kirkridge after spending the night with Sheila and her husband.

Despite ongoing and sometimes seemingly self-inflicted turmoil at his home, Jack maintained his Advisory Board membership at the Earlham School of Religion, but after a few years as chairman of the Prison Chaplaincy and pastor of the Northhampton County Prison, he stepped down in 1987. Jack had been active in the Pennsylvania Prison Society and the Yokefellow Prison Ministry for many years, and his work with ex-convicts, which may have helped many to succeed upon release, ultimately made his last days much more difficult.

After Jane's death, Jack opened his home at Kirkridge as a sort of half-way house for released prisoners. As the years passed, Jack's safety and the safety of the Kirkridge property became worrisome for both his family and friends, and for the Kirkridge Board. One Board member remembers how Jack repeatedly came to them asking to purchase a small portion of the land he still owned to provide ready cash; the member remarks that no one could understand where the money went. It's a good guess that the number of men who lined up at Jack's door for handouts over the years multiplied without Jane's reminding him that his generosity would be his financial ruin.

But a more insidious problem for Jack was the IRS. Because he had to pay taxes on what the land was worth at the time of sale, his taxes soon became unpayable, just as the bills had been over the years. That he was usually selling the land at a loss to a non-profit did not seem to matter. The strain on his heart by the end of the decade left him both weak and dispirited.

What's more, seeing how the direction of Kirkridge had so diverged from his original dream of a movement for power in the Church broke his heart. Friends from Penn State realized how fragile Jack was becoming, and they encouraged him to leave Kirkridge and come to State College. He would be surrounded by loving friends and away from the house guests who had repeatedly stolen from and even assaulted him on more than one occasion.

But Kirkridge was more than his home; it was his legacy. Tsuneo came and stayed for more than a year, and Jack still attended the Company meetings when someone would transport him. At the last Company gathering he attended at Maryland's Dayspring, Jack became short of breath during the Emmaus Walk, which he'd insisted on joining, and Company members discovered that he had forgotten his medication.

In 1988 Jack sent out a lovely Christmas post card that featured a woodcut not of the Nativity but of the Prodigal Son. Beside the woodcut, the card read: "Prodigals, all of us. . .yet in Christmas each is divinely discerned afar, hugged close, given a party. . .Glory! John Oliver Nelson." Jack's summary of his year appears on the reverse side: "Here the Prodigal is a mere teenager but bruised and worn (a woodcut from Global Education Associates)...Less cosmically, 1988 has brought bruises and celebrations (the election included)... Heart attack in May, with brief hospital and 2-1/2 months at posh Buck Hill Inn, guest of the gracious owner...Son Ric's hegira from Hawaii (he paid!) was a delight...Our student went home to Osaka after 20 good months, and there are only 4 houseguests here now... Zest at Chautauqua and Lake Mohonk...Money hurdles and the IRS, AIDS tragedies but not very near...A few pills, concerts, and ballet, too many periodicals, too few prayers, too few reunions with friends far and near: after all what is there but God and friends." What indeed?

The first of the Nelson siblings to die was Jack's younger brother, Doug, a retired minister from New Haven. His death at 76 on November 2, 1989, required Jack to somehow get to Connecticut, and when he arrived for the service, despite their grief over Doug's death, the family was shocked at Jack's disheveled appearance. Sheila's memories of the three-part memorial service for her father reveal a great deal about Jack in those days and for much of his life. Although he arrived disheveled and "almost stunned," Sheila remembers the family wondering how he would ever give the planned eulogy for her father.

But the Jack who stood at the pulpit, she writes, was ..."transformed. He was dynamic, funny, clear; his portion of the service was everything we could have asked, and more. Others there would not have believed the Jack of an hour earlier. He told very funny stories of trips to Scotland that he and my father made, bringing both of them to life as much younger men. He was full of energy and wit, and his memories were very clear. None of us will ever forget what he did."

Jack's Christmas card in 1989 reflects another brief update of his life. Choosing a Kirkridge *Contour* for Advent from a quarter century before, Jack marked the border with red to provide a Christmas spirit. The choice is relevant for Jack's last Christmas card to his many friends, as it speaks of angels and their place in Scripture and in our lives:

"Biblically and now, *any* person sent to give us this assurance [of God's love] is almost indistinguishable from an angel."

And there certainly were angels surrounding Jack in his last months.

On the last page of the booklet, Jack wrote: "Till March 17 I'm at a mid-Pennsylvania retirement village (after two muggings by ex-prisoner junkie friends). I type daily, eat unreservedly, sermonize frequently, rejoice about Eastern Europe, get a frugal trust allowance... Dear brother Doug, 76, died in New Haven; son

Ric is happy in Hawaii, brother Wenley in Gladwyne, sister Peggy Hanson in Rochester... Kirkridge will be 50 in 1992... I exult in my friends...My heart to you!"

The angels in Jack's life carried him to State College after a heart attack in September. Hospitalization was followed by a rehabilitation center, and finally a nursing home in Brookline Village. In the first months, when he felt better, Jack would sneak out of the home to a McDonald's®, never losing his love of a Big Mac®. He celebrated with the Sycamore Community in State College and was visited almost daily by the Roys, the Hawks, Phoebe Link, Kathy Mourant or other friends. Getting his finances in order was their second task after making sure Jack lived in a safe place. This was accomplished again through the help of those angels in his life from State College and beyond.

In January 1990 Jack was hospitalized again with a perforated duodenal ulcer. This was a major operation and set him back health wise. When he returned to the nursing home, Jack was confined to a wheelchair in the assisted living community at Brookline. His niece Sheila, her brother Doug, her stepmother Jerry, and her cousin John Nelson came to visit him one Sunday that winter

Sheila recalled a vivid memory of the visit. "We walked into the lobby, which was open to the dining area," she remembered. Walking to the reception desk, they asked if they could see Jack Nelson. "The receptionist pointed to a table in the dining area," she writes. "There was only one person there, a figure in a hooded bathrobe slumped over the table. He could not have looked more desolate. None of us could even speak at first, we were so stunned." And the most remarkable part of the story happened after that initial meeting. Jack said that he wanted to dress and call some of his friends to join them. The group toured the grounds for a while "almost too stunned to speak," and when they returned, Jack was "transformed." Dressed as they had all remembered him in dress pants, white shirt and tie, Jack had arranged for a conference room that would accommodate a larger group. The Roys, Phoebe Link, Ernie and Jean Hawk arrived, and "Jack presided as though he were a CEO introducing seminar participants, absolutely in charge."

His last Christmas was spent with Phoebe and Bob Link, but even at Brookline, Jack never gave up his ministry. On December 11, 1989, he sent a cover letter to Janice Grana in Nashville, apologizing for not meeting the deadline for a week's lectionary meditations for the Upper Room *Disciplines 1991*, but he still completed them. "More of your readers may know me as 'longtime professor, Yale Divinity School' than as a founder of Kirkridge," Jack wrote; "use your own judgment about that by-line." He called his week's meditations: *God Through a Person and a People.*

One of the most interesting reflections about Jack's last days was written six years after his death by Ernie Hawk, a friend of many decades, who was there at the end. Jack was "a lousy patient," he writes. "The urbane, kindly, caring JON we all had known and loved exited early, leaving a cranky sub-personality to mop up the last few weeks and days." This unsettling remembrance, however, prompted Ernie to realize that Jack had a certain "impatience with dying," adding, "He sensed the end was in sight and he wanted to go."

A further breakthrough in understanding those last days came when Ernie remembered the ceramic tile of Thomas Carlyle's Candle, which Jack had placed in the fireplace of the Lodge at Kirkridge, the first building in the pursuit of his dream. The Latin inscription, *Terar dum prosim*, is often translated "Let me be consumed, provided I be of use."

Jack had lived life to the full, "burning the candle down to the last bit of wick," Ernie writes. "What we observed in those last days was the sputtering out of that life so grandly spent. He gave until there was no more to give. He was spent and impatient to go."

A letter dated April 15 sent to Jack's many friends relates how on the Saturday before his Monday death, the Sycamore Community held a celebrative communion service in his room. Jack managed to hum bits of the bass with Ernie Hawk's tenor of the Scottish psalter version of the 23rd Psalm. He passed on the blessing of life to little six-month-old Ethan, the youngest member of the Sycamore Community: "It was a touching, symbolic passing of the baton." His dear friend Phoebe Link was called to come to the nursing home on April 9, and leaving the school where she was teaching, she arrived at his room and realized that Jack's translation into eternity was over. "After prayer, I found myself singing aloud the famous hymn, 'To Be a Pilgrim,'" she writes. It was Phoebe who signed the Certificate of Death.

Word of Jack's death spread through word of mouth and obituaries in local and national periodicals, including the *New York Times.* Phone calls and letters arrived at Kirkridge with tributes to this man who had influenced so many over the years.

A memorial service was held to celebrate Jack's life on June 16, 1990 at the Kirkridge Lodge, which today bears his name. Before his death, Jack chose much of the content of his memorial service, put together by his friends in the Sycamore Community. His niece Sheila received his ashes, as she had also been given the mahogany box containing Jane's cremains. She planned to bury the ashes together in the Nelson family plot, as requested in Jack's will. Not having a death certificate for Jane, however, she could not fulfill that request until this book was begun and the certificate retrieved from a funeral home in Saskatoon.

A liturgy of committal was finally held on September 23, 1995 in Homewood Cemetery, Pittsburgh, Pennsylvania, and a memorial stone in Jack's honor was placed near the Lodge, a gift of family and friends. At each of these memorial events the Kirkridge Prayer, so loved by Jack, was recited:

The Kirkridge Prayer

Almighty Father, known in our silence and entreated in our hunger for Thee, nourish us now with the common bread of Thy grace. Shape with Thy hands the witness of this quiet company, that our ministry may be Christ's own life in our day. Bestow Thy serenity and clean strength on each friend of Kirkridge, granting us honest work and steadfast friendship in Him. Deepen, O God, Thy intention for our life in Thee. Through Christ our Lord. Amen.

44.-45. Grave markers of Rev. John Oliver and Rev. Jane Bone
Nelson at the Homewood Cemetery in Pittsburgh, Pennsylvania

46. Rustum Roy at Interment of the Nelson
Cremains, Sept. 23, 1995.

47. Nelson family burial plot at Homewood Cemetery
in Pittsburgh, PA. Markers for John and Jane Nelson
at foot of Celtic Cross reads John Evon Nelson 1879-
1953, Margaret Dodds Nelson 1880-1966

"Biography is the mesh through which our real life escapes."

~ Tom Stoppard (***The Invention of Love*** 1997)

Epilogue

No biography can do justice to a life. I knew John Oliver Nelson from 1976 until his death in 1990. Having come to Kirkridge for the first time in August of that year for the Company at Kirkridge Inaugural Event, I was chosen to be a member of the Steering Committee and remained active in the Company for the years that it grew and then waned. My affiliation with this group of dedicated Christians and the man who envisioned it profoundly influenced my life.

When his friends asked me to write a biography of Jack a few years after his death, I had no idea that the project would become as time-consuming and complicated as it turned out to be. Although Jack Nelson died two decades ago this year, and many who knew and loved him are now gone, his story and legacy deserve to be shared with the world.

John Oliver Nelson was an extraordinary man. A visionary, a dreamer, dapper, quick-witted, intelligent, and charming, Jack loved liturgy, music, and the fine arts. He loved the ministry. He loved words, and his letters and diaries are filled with Scottish expressions, obviously a dialect of English that he acquired from his earliest years. Personal letters were almost always signed "Yours aye," and his years of study in Scotland and association with Sir George MacLeod and Iona were the seeds that blossomed into Kirkridge in 1942.

Jack was also a very complicated man. He began life in a home that seemed to have completely escaped the Depression, and then spent the rest of his life giving money away as if it burned a hole in his pockets. Much of his inheritance, based on Gulf Oil stocks, built the buildings at Kirkridge and kept it afloat in the early years.

Another large percentage went to people who were down and out, addicted to drugs and alcohol, unable to hold down or procure jobs, pay their rent, or feed their families. Some of it went to what we might call the "undeserving poor." But for Jack, the mandate of the Gospel to feed the hungry, clothe the naked, and shelter the homeless made no distinctions. His faith in perhaps changing the hearts and lives of many of these supplicants inspired him to give until he had nothing material left to give. He enfleshed Philippians 2:7: Like Christ, he "emptied himself."

Jack's commitment to Incarnational Theology, a doctrine that professes that Christ reveals himself to us in the mundane as well as the resplendent in our everyday lives, permeated Kirkridge and his life. In the early years, Kirkridge was founded to provide a space for young clergymen, mainly Presbyterian as was Jack, whom he called "square pegs," men who didn't easily fit the mold of the average seminary experience. He hoped to send these ministers to rural areas, poorer regions of cities, and missions across the globe. Many of these seminarians, in fact, lived out this vision upon ordination. If Jack was an academic, whose years at Yale and Ph.D. gave him a certain prominence, he was also an evangelist, a preacher whose words are still remembered by the thousands who heard him preach or read his *Contours* or *Ridgeleafs* or the books he managed to get to the publisher between retreats or meetings of the myriad organizations he headed or belonged to.

Yes, other rich men have given their money away. Many attempt to live out the Christian message in their daily lives. What makes John Oliver Nelson worthy of such adulation?

In many respects, he was a failure. SAKI, the school that he dreamed of building to give young people a values-centered liberal arts education, lasted only two years. Turning Point was built to provide a rehabilitation center for those addicted to alcohol and drugs, again with an emphasis on Christianity. That, too, lasted only a few years. The chapel that he wanted to build on the mountain never materialized. He couldn't leave an endowment to keep his beloved Kirkridge solvent because he had nothing in his bank account. So what should we glean from his life?

First of all, he gave us Kirkridge. It's easy to see this as a retreat center, a collection of buildings on a mountain in the Poconos, but it was never just that. Jack founded Kirkridge as a movement for power in the Church. If he was a committed Presbyterian minister, over the years he embraced other denominations of Christians, even the Roman Catholics he referred to as RCs in his diaries.

I remember the many times that Jack talked about the Church-types and the sect-types, those who closely identified with the institutional Church and those whose concept of Church was the broader understanding of Church as the people of God. That broadness of vision, the embracing of all, allowed Kirkridge to be a welcoming place for Christian gays and lesbians, a legacy that remains to this day.

When the Company was founded, the brochure for that Inaugural Event had a dove on the cover with the words from Isaiah: "Behold, I am doing a new thing." The Company was designed, as was Kirkridge, to level the playing field between clergy and laity, Protestant and Catholic, men and women, gay and straight. All were welcome here—and that was a new thing inspired by Jack's openness to the new.

In the Sixties Kirkridge became a place where Christians could discuss sexuality openly, where peacemaking was promulgated in the midst of war. Kirkridge was always ahead of the curve, always trying to explore issues that many Churches found too controversial. It was an open space, a non-judgmental atmosphere. And Jack and later Jane Nelson, made it that way from the beginning.

Now a decade into the 21st century, Kirkridge once again struggles with its vision. The world of 1942 that inspired those "hungry young men" to take the Gospel message and spread it to every nation is a very different world. Jack often spoke of the "unchurched" in the early days of the Company.

In the recent Pew Research Forum on Religion and Public Life Report, "Religion Among the Millennials" (www.pewforum.org), we learn that a full 25% of young Americans between 18 and 29 do not affiliate themselves with any religion. A mere third attend church services at least once a week. Fewer young people say that religion is very important in their lives, and they tend to pray more than the same age group in the 1980s, claiming to be spiritual but not religious.

What does it mean then to Picket and Pray in the 21st century? What future does the Church have if these young people do not affiliate themselves with any church?

Given the economic collapse of the nation in the past few years, two wars abroad and civil unrest at home, what would John Oliver Nelson aspire to if Kirkridge were his dream today? Although part of an educated elite, Jack always identified himself with what the Gospel refers to as the "least" among the brethren. With ecclesiastical structures of every denomination to upkeep, is it any wonder that the average sermon on a given Sunday does not speak of peacemaking, or sharing the wealth with the "least" of the nation, of support for equality in the workplace or the society in general?

Church-types, for Jack Nelson, have a similar mission, but their message is often muted by what ministers see as the reality of the situation. There are bills to be paid, and they are not usually paid for by the poorest of their congregations.

Jack surely experienced this in 1942, and he began a new movement for power in the Church. He asked first that those early Kirkridgers make an accounting of their time and money. The Company began with much the same vision—yet the cost of discipleship was high, and just as the number of early Kirkridgers who kept the Kirkridge discipline waned, so did the number of Company members who began in earnest but eventually saw the Company merely as a committed group of friends, who enjoyed each other's company and kept Jack's spirit alive through occasional meetings and communication with one another.

Remembering John Oliver Nelson a century after his birth is a call to revisit his vision, to ask the questions of this society that he asked of his, to ask of ourselves what we are willing to do to promote the movement for power in the Church.

How will we picket and pray in this new century? The world may be different, yet the call to discipleship is always the same. Kirkridge historically had a prophetic role to play in the Church, and those of us who have been inspired by Jack Nelson's vision over the years have that same role: to enter into the issues of our day with energy and reflection that is Gospel-based, committed to Christ, and open to the world.

Rita M. Yeasted

Hymn sung at John Oliver Nelson's
48. Memorial Service

BE THOU MY VISION, O LORD

SLANE. 10. 10. 10. 10.

Ancient Irish; tr. by MARY BYRNE
Versified by ELEANOR HULL
Unison. Moderately slow, with great dignity

Ancient Irish traditional melody
Harmonized by DAVID EVANS, 1874–

1. Be Thou my Vi - sion, O Lord of my heart;
2. Be Thou my Wis - dom, and Thou my true Word;
3. Rich - es I heed not, nor seek hu - man praise,
4. High Queen of heav - en, my vic - to - ry won,

Naught be all else to me, save that Thou art—
I ev - er with Thee and Thou with me, Lord;
Thou mine in - her - it - ance, now and al - ways:
May I reach heav - en's joys, O bright heaven's Sun!

Thou my best thought, by day or by night,
Thou my great Mo - ther, I Thy true son;
Thou and Thou on - ly, first in my heart,
Heart of my own heart, what - ev - er be - fall,

Wak - ing or sleep - ing, Thy pres - ence my light.
Thou in me dwell - ing, and I with Thee one.
High King of heav - en, my treas - ure Thou art.
Still be my Vi - sion, O Rul - er of all. A - MEN.

172

Selected Bibliography

Books written or edited by John Oliver Nelson

America Inherits Religion. **Chicago: Delphian Society, 1940.**

A Bibliography on the Laity. **New Haven: World Council of Churches, 1959.**

The Christian Conscience and War: A Statement by Theologians and Religious Leaders. **Scottdale, PA: Herald , n.d. (Church Peace Mission Pamphlet—with introduction by John Oliver Nelson)**

Dare to Reconcile: **Seven Settings for Creating Community. New York: Association, 1946.**

Every Occupation a Christian Calling. **New York: Association, 1951.**

A Listing of Church Vocations. **New York: National Council of Churches, 1958-1967.**

Look at the Ministry (A Message in Photos). **Community on Ministry, Federal Council of Churches. New York: Association, 1946-7.**

Rita M. Yeasted

Opportunities in Protestant Religious Vocations. **New York: VGM, 1952.**

Opportunities in Religious Service Careers. **Series. Skokie: VGM, 1980-88.**

Possibly the Ministry? **New York: National Council of Churches, n.d.**

Reconciliation and the Powers of This World. **n.p., 1967.**

The Rise of the Princeton Theology: A Genetic Study of American Presbyterianism until 1850. **Ann Arbor: University Microfilms, 1976. (Yale Dissertation)**

The Student Prayerbook. **Haddam House. New York: Association, 1953.**

Vocation and Protestant Religious Occupations. **New York: VGM, 1963.**

We Have This Ministry: Church Vocations for Men and Women. **New York: Association, 1946.**

Work and Vocation: A Christian Discussion. **New York: Harper, 1954. (Edited with an introduction by John Oliver Nelson)**

Young Laymen—Young Church: A Summons to Young Laymen in the Mid-Twentieth Century. **New York: Association, 1948.**

Audiocassettes and Video Recordings

"The Christian and His Vocation." Eugene Carson Blake, John Oliver Nelson, and others. Videorecording, 1994. (Housed at Union Presbyterian School of Christian Education, Morgan Library, Richmond, Va.)

"Consider Your Call." Cassette tape. 1956. (Housed at Union PSCE, Morgan Library.)

"Look at Women's Church Vocations." Filmstrip. Chicago: Society for Visual Education. 1970.

"The Miracle of Prayer." Cassette tape. Atlanta: TRAV, 1968. (Housed at Union PSCE.)

"Piety in a World Come of Age." Cassette tape. 1966. (Housed at Union PSCE.)

"Vocation: Every Christian's Business." Cassette tape. 1956. (Housed at Union PSCE.)

Other Books/Items of Interest

Clark, Henry. *The Christian Case Against Poverty.* New York: Association. 1965.

Go Tell It on the Mountain: Stories of Kirkridge 1942-1992. Bangor: Kirkridge, 1992.

"John Oliver Nelson: Cleric Who Founded Ecumenical Retreat." *New York Times* (online obituary) 17 April 1990.

Rita M. Yeasted

MacLeod, George. *We Shall Rebuild: The Work of the Iona Community on Mainland and on Island.* **Philadelphia: Kirkridge, 1949.**

McNeill, John. *Both Feet Planted Firmly in Mid-Air: My Spiritual Journey.* **Louisville. Westminster/John Knox. 1998.**

Roy, Rustum and Della Roy. *Honest Sex: A Revolutionary Sex Ethic by and for Concerned Christians.* **Bangor, PA: Kirkridge, 1968.**

Toffler, Alvin. *Future Shock.* **New York: Random House. 1970.**

Weaver, Fred J. *Fishers of Men: History of Brentwood Presbyterian Church: 40th Anniversary--1969.* **n.p. 1969.**

You're Alright, Jack. **Bangor: Kirkridge, 1975.**

List of Photographs

20. Jane Bone and her father, John Bone, on the day of her wedding
21. Doug, Wenley, Georgina, Jack, Jane, Mr. & Mrs. Bone, Margaret, May Young (Reverend's wife), Reverend Arthur Young, UCC
22. Nelson family photo: Jack, Jane, and Rick
23. Darwood (early Nelson residence) at Kirkridge March 29, 1959. In the circle (left to right): Edith Platt, Irme and Fritz van der Bent, George Buciarski, JON, Ans van der Bent, Joseph Platt, Pete Ingalls (back of heads in foreground)
24-25. Jack and Jane Nelson vacationing in Acapulco, Mexico aboard SS Fiesta on January 15, 1966
26. JON and Jane at Hotel El Presidente, Acapulco on January 18, 1966 with Sidney Francis Smith III
27. Jack and his mother Margaret on a cruise, December. 20, 1957
28. John Oliver Nelson (JON) looking to horizon through window of the Lodge.
29. JON addressing the Scranton Council of Churches, October 19, 1968
30. Scranton Council of Churches meeting October 19, 1968
31. Jack and Walter Dend (of Corning) at Eriskay
32. "Tobermory" 1972 (now Turning Point's sleeping quarters)
33. Jane Nelson, Douglas and Dorothy Steere in 1973
34. "Mull" November 1975 (now the Nelson Lodge sleeping quarters)
35. SAKI reunion on June 19, 1976 (Jack on right, first row)
36. "Tea and Symphony" at Jack and Jane Nelson's Tiree dining room in Tiree.
37-38. Jack and Jane Nelson shoveling snow at Tiree (their home at Kirkridge), March 1978
39. Dan Berrigan's annual retreat at Kirkridge, January 1979
40. Jane Bone Nelson, May 1980

41. Dayspring Retreat led by Jack Nelson on May 3, 1980
42. Jack and Jane Nelson, Margaret Bone Leaker, and Ella Bone in July 1980
43. Sexuality Workshop on August 24, 1980. Participants in photo include Muriel McGlamery, M.D., JON, an unidentified participant, Della Roy, Rustum Roy, Anne Stewart, Jane Nelson, and Georgina Bone.
44. Grave markers of Rev. John Oliver and Rev. Jane Bone Nelson at the Homewood Cemetery in Pittsburgh, Pennsylvania
45. Grave markers of Rev. John Oliver and Rev. Jane Bone Nelson at the Homewood Cemetery in Pittsburgh, Pennsylvania
46. Rustum Roy at Interment of the Nelson Cremains, Sept. 23, 1995.
47. Nelson family burial plot at Homewood Cemetery in Pittsburgh, PA. Markers for John and Jane Nelson at foot of Celtic Cross reads John Evon Nelson 1879-1953, Margaret Dodds Nelson 1880-1966
48. "Be Thou My Vision": Hymn sung at John Oliver Nelson's Memorial Service

Index

Bone, John, 83 (death)
Bone, Mary Campbell, 109 (death)
Hanson, Howard, 145 (death)
McBride, Elizabeth Nelson, 143-4 (death), 144 (memorial)
Nelson, Rev. Douglas, 160 (death), 160 (funeral)
Nelson, Rev. Jane Bone, 148 (death), 150 (Kirkridge memorial),
    163 (Homewood memorial)
Nelson, John Evon, 36 (death)
Nelson, John Oliver, 163 (death), 163 (Kirkridge memorial), 163
    (Homewood memorial)
Nelson, Margaret Dodds, 73 (death), 74 (funeral)
Nelson, Mary Forsythe, 85 (death)
Nelson, Wera, 113 (death), 113 (memorial)
Ecumenical Efforts, 9, 59, 75
Education, 4
Engagement to Jane, 48
Formation of Company at Kirkridge, 110-113
Influences:
    Church of the Saviour, 42-3
    Gore, Bishop Charles (Church of England), 14
    Fellowship of Reconciliation, 15
    Iona, 7-9, 35-6
    MacLeod, Sir George, 7-8, 14, 35
    Oxford Group, 24
    Platt, Joseph and Edith, 37-43
    Princeton Crusaders, 6, 24
    Quakers, 19
    Taize Community, 15
    Talbot House, 14
    TOC H, 14
    Young Men's Christian Association (YMCA), 4, 31
Kirkridge:
    "American Iona," 13, 15, 62, 97
    As a movement, 17-8, 22-3, 25, 37, 40-1, 43, 58, 64-5, 110, 119,
    159, 169-71
    Begins Lectionary, 24
    Cell formation, 24-5
    Center for art and music, 36, 61-2, 82, 134
    Choice of location, 15-6
    Choice of name, 18
    Contours begun, 24

Nelson, Roma (Wenley's wife), 124, 132, 146, 151
Nelson, Wenley Dodds (brother), viii, xii (photo), 3-4, 6, 10
(photo), 49, 50 (photo), 74, 106, 112-3, 118, 124-5, 131-2, 135,
141, 145-7, 151, 153, 155-61, 177-8
Nelson, Wera (Wenley's wife), 106, 112, 113 (death)
New Windsor Service Center (Maryland), 127
"Next Thirty Years Fund," 98
Nichols, Dr. David H. (surgeon), 124
Northern Ireland Peace Movement, 114-5
Nouwen, Henri, 127, 146, 150

O
Oak Street Project, 43
Oaten, Rev. Beverly (Five Oaks), 49
Oxford Group (later Moral Re-Armament), 24

P
Paradise, Scott, 68
Pareis, Eric, 156-7
Pendle Hill (Quaker), 19, 36, 72, 94, 97
Pennington, Dom Basil, OCSO, 105
Pennsylvania College for Women (now Chatham University), 2
Pennsylvania Prison Society, 158
Pennsylvania State University (Penn State), vii, 27, 38, 61, 79, 90,
94-5, 159
"Picket and Pray," 17, 25, 37, 43, 110, 170-1
Pittsburgh Theological Seminary, 1, 60, 74
Platt, Edith, 37-8, 40-3, 58, 63 (photo), 106, 178
Platt, Joseph, 37-8, 40-4, 58, 63 (photo), 106, 178
Pope, Liston (Yale Divinity Dean), 49
Presbyterian Board of Christian Education, 15, 24, 30
Presbyterian Peace Fellowship, 55, 120
Princeton University, 4-7, 24, 46, 47 (photo), 52, 59, 107, 121, 125,
129, 137
Prophecy (Saint Columba), 9

Protestant Retreat Movement, vii